Gooseberry Patch ™

A Country Store In Your Mailbox℠

Celebrate Winter
...fireside feasts and merry celebrations

A Country Store In Your Mailbox®

Gooseberry Patch
P.O. Box 190, Dept. CELW
Delaware, OH 43015

1-800-85-GOOSE
1-800-854-6673

Copyright 1996, Gooseberry Patch
1-888052-01-5
First Printing 30,000 copies, June, 1996

How To Subscribe

Would you like to receive
"A Country Store in Your Mailbox"® ?
For a 2-year subscription to our
Gooseberry Patch catalog
simply send $3.00 to:
Gooseberry Patch
P.O. Box 190, Dept. CELW
Delaware, OH 43015

Printed in the United States of America
TOOF COOKBOOK DIVISION

670 South Cooper Street
Memphis, TN 38104

Contents

Dedication

To everyone who has ever
discovered joy
in a snowy day, a crackling fire,
a Christmas carol or a freshly-baked pie.

Appreciation

To all of our Gooseberry Family
whose memories and laughter
keep us warm throughout the year.

Comfort Foods

...soothing your way on a long winter's night

Golden Baked Macaroni and Cheese
Homemade Meat Loaf
Mike's Grandma's Chili
Creamy Chicken a la King
Toasted Barley Casserole
Steamy Winter Vegetable Stew
Comforting Chicken Noodle Soup
Homestyle Swiss Steak
Fluffy Mashed Potatoes
Spicy Ham Loaf
Angel Hair Pasta with Lemon and Basil
Thick, Juicy Burgers
Skinny Linguine with Hot 'n Spicy Shrimp Sauce
Caramel Pecan Cheesecake
Chocolate Mousse Fantasy

*I heard a bird sing
In the dark of December
A magical thing
And sweet to remember.
"We are nearer to spring
than we were in September,"
I heard a bird sing
In the Dark of December.*

— Oliver Herford

Golden Baked Macaroni and Cheese

Warm memories of childhood!

2 lb. elbow macaroni
1 c. melted butter
7 c. milk

1 1/2 to 2 lb. sharp cheddar
cheese, cut into chunks
salt and freshly ground
pepper to taste

Cook macaroni in boiling water until about 2/3 of the way done. Drain and rinse well under cold running water to stop the cooking process. In a large roasting pan, toss macaroni with the butter and season with salt and pepper. Mix the cheese in thoroughly with a wooden spoon. Pour in enough milk to barely cover the macaroni. Bake, uncovered, in a pre-heated 350 degree oven for about 1/2 hour or until the cheese starts to melt; then stir well. Taste and adjust seasonings. Cook for another hour, until macaroni is beginning to brown and all milk has been absorbed.

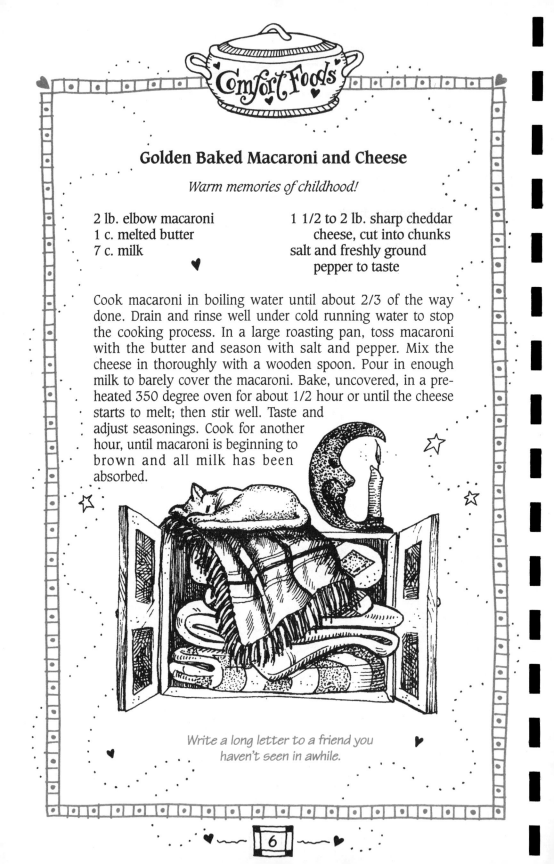

Write a long letter to a friend you haven't seen in awhile.

Homemade Meat Loaf

Tastes like it came right out of Mom's oven.

1 lb. ground chuck
1 lb. ground veal
1 lb. ground pork
2 c. bread crumbs
2 eggs, lightly beaten
salt and pepper to taste
1 or 2 garlic cloves,
    crushed

1/4 c. dry red wine
1/2 c. fresh parsley,
    chopped
28 oz. can plum tomatoes,
    drained and crushed
    (reserve juice)

Combine all ingredients except juice from tomatoes in a large bowl and gently mix with your hands. Add 2/3 of the tomato juice and combine well. In a shallow baking dish, form the meat into a plump loaf, about 8" long x 4" high. Bake in 350 degree oven for 1 to 1 1/2 hours, or until a meat thermometer registers 170 degrees. Allow to cool 1/2 hour before slicing.

Browse through your baby pictures or high school yearbook for a humorous pick-me-up!

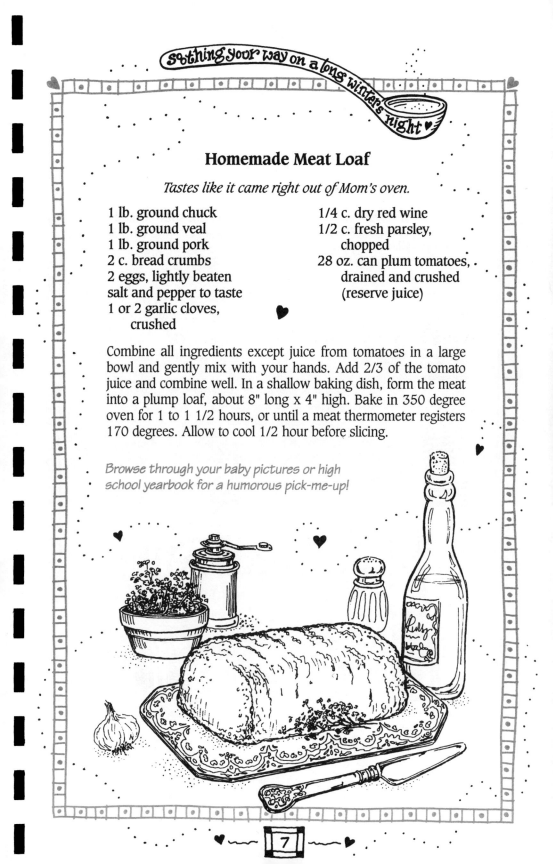

Mike's Grandma's Chili

Add more chili powder to make it as hot as you like!

1 lb. ground beef
1 c. onions, chopped
1 clove garlic, minced
16 oz. can kidney beans
1 qt. tomato juice
1/2 t. ground cumin

1 t. chili powder
1 t. salt
1/2 t. pepper
1 t. oregano
1/2 c. brown sugar

In a large soup pot, brown onion, garlic and ground beef until meat is browned and crumbly. Add all other ingredients and simmer on low for 30 minutes or longer.

*Next to jazz music, there is nothing that
lifts the spirit and strengthens the soul
more than a good bowl of chili.*
- Harry James

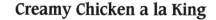

Creamy Chicken a la King

This hearty dish can also be served over rice, mashed potatoes or hot biscuits!

5 T. sweet butter
1 c. fresh mushrooms, sliced
1/2 red bell pepper, seeded and diced
3/4 c. fresh or frozen peas
1/4 c. flour
32 oz. can chicken broth

3 c. cooked chicken, cubed
1/2 c. sliced carrots, cooked
1 T. fresh parsley, minced
salt and pepper to taste
8 oz. wide egg noodles, cooked

Sauté mushrooms in butter until tender and set aside. Cook bell pepper and peas in small pan of boiling water for 2 minutes and rinse in cold water. In a separate saucepan, melt 4 tablespoons. of butter, sprinkle the flour over the butter and stir with a fork until smooth, about 2 minutes. Slowly add most of the chicken broth, whisking thoroughly. Simmer until thick, about 5 minutes. Add chicken, carrots, mushrooms in butter, pepper, peas, cooked carrots, parsley and seasonings. Simmer another 5 minutes, thinning with additional chicken broth if it becomes too thick. Serve over hot buttered noodles. Serves 4.

Toasted Barley Casserole

*The beef broth soaked into the barley
makes this a most satisfying dish!*

1 c. pearl barley, rinsed
1/2 c. pine nuts
3 T. butter, divided
1/2 c. parsley, chopped

1/4 c. green onions, minced
1/4 t. salt
1/4 t. freshly ground pepper
3 c. beef broth, heated

Toast pine nuts in 1 tablespoon butter, remove from skillet and
set aside. Add remaining butter to skillet, add onion and barley,
and stir until barley is toasted. Stir in nuts, parsley, onion and
seasonings. Spoon into 1 1/2 qt. casserole. Pour hot broth over
casserole and mix well. Bake, uncovered, 90 minutes in 375
degree oven. Garnish with fresh parsley.

Steamy Winter Vegetable Stew

Hearty and healthful!

4 c. water
2 cubes chicken bouillon
1 lb. carrots, cut into chunks
1/2 head cauliflower,
    separated into flowerets

1 large acorn squash, peeled,
    seeded and cut into 1"
    cubes
1/2 lb. Brussels sprouts, cut
    in half lengthwise
3 T. butter
1/4 c. flour

Heat water and bouillon cubes to a boil. Add
carrots, cover, and cook for 10 minutes.
Add cauliflower and cook 5 minutes
longer. Add squash and cook a few minutes longer. Add sprouts and cook
until tender. Drain vegetables, reserving 3 cups of cooking liquid. Melt butter in a saucepan and stir in flour. Cook
until mixture is bubbly; then gradually
stir in cooking liquid. Continue to stir
until thickened. Return vegetables to
the saucepan and stir to combine
with the sauce.

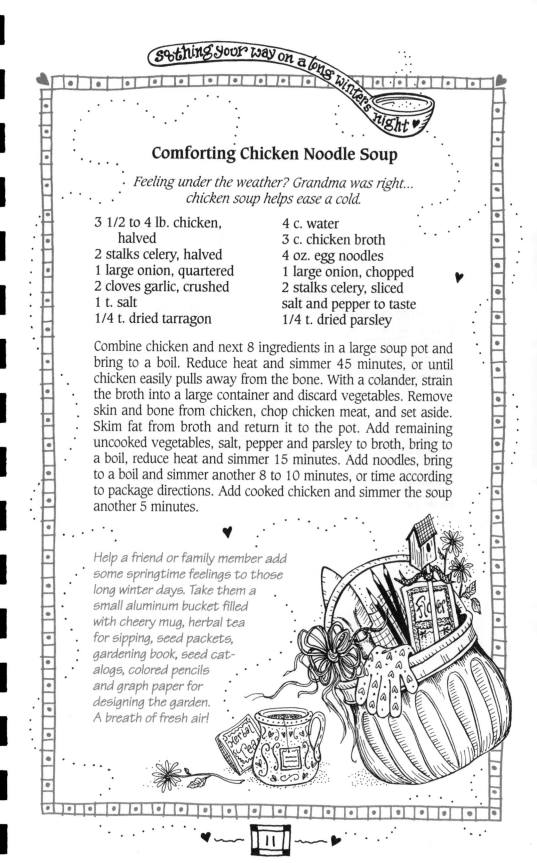

Comforting Chicken Noodle Soup

Feeling under the weather? Grandma was right...
chicken soup helps ease a cold.

3 1/2 to 4 lb. chicken,
   halved
2 stalks celery, halved
1 large onion, quartered
2 cloves garlic, crushed
1 t. salt
1/4 t. dried tarragon

4 c. water
3 c. chicken broth
4 oz. egg noodles
1 large onion, chopped
2 stalks celery, sliced
salt and pepper to taste
1/4 t. dried parsley

Combine chicken and next 8 ingredients in a large soup pot and bring to a boil. Reduce heat and simmer 45 minutes, or until chicken easily pulls away from the bone. With a colander, strain the broth into a large container and discard vegetables. Remove skin and bone from chicken, chop chicken meat, and set aside. Skim fat from broth and return it to the pot. Add remaining uncooked vegetables, salt, pepper and parsley to broth, bring to a boil, reduce heat and simmer 15 minutes. Add noodles, bring to a boil and simmer another 8 to 10 minutes, or time according to package directions. Add cooked chicken and simmer the soup another 5 minutes.

Help a friend or family member add some springtime feelings to those long winter days. Take them a small aluminum bucket filled with cheery mug, herbal tea for sipping, seed packets, gardening book, seed catalogs, colored pencils and graph paper for designing the garden. A breath of fresh air!

Homestyle Swiss Steak

This fork-tender dish is full of rich, flavorful gravy.

2 T. flour
1/4 t. salt
1/4 t. pepper
2 lb. round steak, cut into
    1" strips

1 onion, chopped
2 stalks of celery, chopped
15 oz. can stewed tomatoes
2 T. Worcestershire sauce

Combine flour, salt and pepper. Dredge beef strips in the mixture and set aside. In large skillet, melt butter and sauté onion and celery for 2 minutes. Add beef to skillet and brown on both sides. Stir in tomatoes with liquid and Worcestershire sauce. Simmer, covered, over low heat for 60 to 90 minutes, until beef is very tender. Add water if necessary to thin the gravy. Serve with mashed potatoes.

Fluffy Mashed Potatoes

There are times when a mound of mashed potatoes, hot from the pan with the butter melting down, is the only thing that will satisfy.

5 baking potatoes
1/4 c. evaporated milk

5 T. unsalted butter
salt and pepper to taste

Scrub potatoes and boil in their jackets in a large pot of boiling salted water. Cook about 30 minutes, or until fork-tender. Remove potatoes, rinse under cold water, and peel. Boil the cooking water down to about 1 quart. While potato water is boiling, cut potatoes into quarters and mash in a large pan with a potato masher. (Mashing the potatoes as well as possible before adding remaining ingredients will keep them fluffy.) Add a cup of the potato water and continue to mash over a low burner. Add the butter, seasonings and evaporated milk and beat until fluffy.

Spicy Ham Loaf

Serve with baked yams and applesauce.

1lb. ground ham and 1/2 lb.
  ground fresh pork
1 egg
1 t. cloves, ground

1 T. brown sugar
1 c. bread crumbs
1/2 c. milk

Mix all ingredients together and form into a loaf. Bake uncovered in preheated 350 degree oven for 30 minutes. Then adjust temperature to 325 and bake an additional 30 minutes.

While baking, baste with a mixture of:

1/4 c. vinegar
1/4 c. water

♥ 1/2 c. brown sugar, packed
1/2 t. dry or brown
  prepared mustard

Angel Hair Pasta with Lemon and Basil

Quick-cooking angel hair pasta will satisfy your craving in the blink of an eye!

6 oz. angel hair pasta
1/4 c. fresh basil leaves, chopped
1/4 c. lemon juice
Parmesan cheese, freshly grated

1 T. grated lemon peel
3 T. olive oil
1/2 t. black pepper

Cook pasta 3 to 5 minutes in boiling water. Drain. Toss with remaining ingredients, reserving cheese to sprinkle on top.

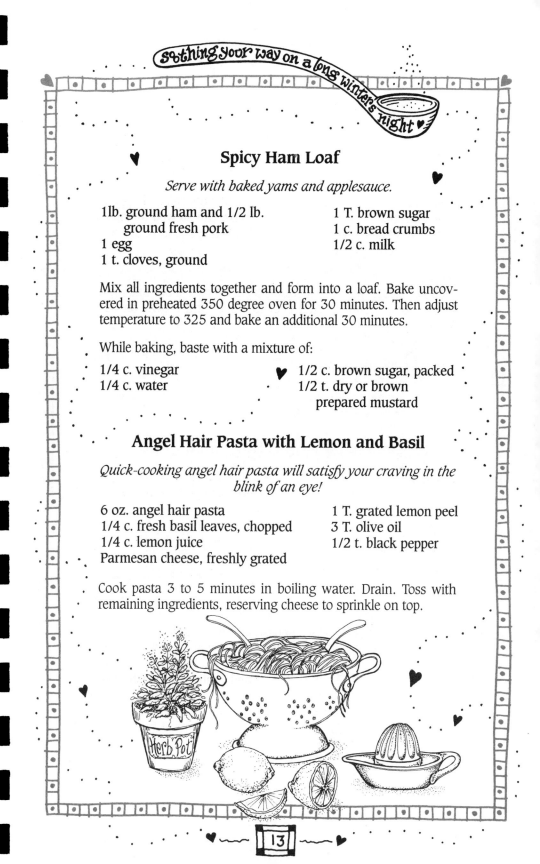

Thick, Juicy Burgers

Add a slice of American cheese for double satisfaction.

1/2 lb. ground chuck
1/4 t. dried onion flakes
salt

1 t. ice water
freshly ground pepper to
  taste

With wet hands, gently mix ice water, onion flakes and pepper into the ground chuck and form into two patties, each about 1/2" thick. Be careful not to pack the meat too tightly, as this will make tough, dried-out burgers. Sprinkle salt on an iron skillet and heat over medium-high heat until a drop of water bounces off the surface. Carefully drop the patties onto the skillet, allowing them to brown for 30 seconds before lowering heat to medium-low. Cook for an additional 3 minutes and turn. Do not smash the patties with your spatula, as this will release all the juice. Cook 4 to 5 minutes longer, until meat is done the way you like it. Serve on toasted buns with your choice of condiments.

Skinny Linguine with Hot 'n Spicy Shrimp

*Go ahead...indulge! This hearty, spicy, fat-free dish
will be a favorite.*

2 T. olive oil
1 clove garlic, minced
1/3 c. onion, diced
1/2 lb. fresh raw shrimp,
  shelled and deveined
1/4 t. red pepper flakes,
  crushed

6 oz. can evaporated skim
  milk
8 oz. can tomato sauce
1 c. fresh or canned
  tomatoes, diced & drained
1/4 c. white wine
4 to 6 oz. linguine, cooked

Sauté onion and garlic in olive oil until transparent. Add shrimp and sauté for about 3 minutes, or until white. Sprinkle with red pepper. Stir in skim milk, tomato sauce, tomatoes and white wine, stirring constantly. Serve over hot cooked linguine. Serves 2 as a main dish; 4 as a side dish.

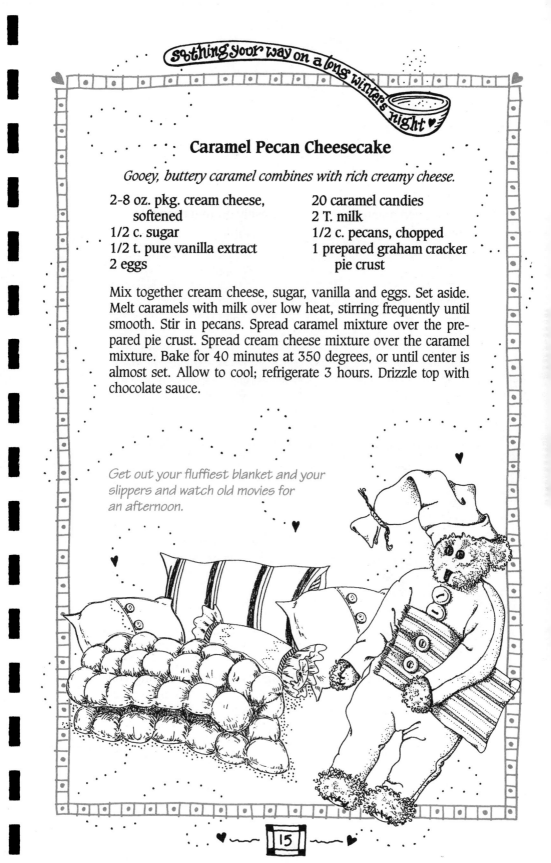

Caramel Pecan Cheesecake

Gooey, buttery caramel combines with rich creamy cheese.

2-8 oz. pkg. cream cheese,
    softened
1/2 c. sugar
1/2 t. pure vanilla extract
2 eggs

20 caramel candies
2 T. milk
1/2 c. pecans, chopped
1 prepared graham cracker
    pie crust

Mix together cream cheese, sugar, vanilla and eggs. Set aside. Melt caramels with milk over low heat, stirring frequently until smooth. Stir in pecans. Spread caramel mixture over the prepared pie crust. Spread cream cheese mixture over the caramel mixture. Bake for 40 minutes at 350 degrees, or until center is almost set. Allow to cool; refrigerate 3 hours. Drizzle top with chocolate sauce.

Get out your fluffiest blanket and your slippers and watch old movies for an afternoon.

Chocolate Mousse Fantasy

Creamy. Chocolatey. Sinfully rich!

6 oz. white chocolate	1 egg
2 t. butter	1 egg yolk
1 c. walnuts, finely chopped	1/2 c. heavy cream, very
6 oz. semi-sweet chocolate,	hot but not boiling
broken	2 T. dark rum
2 T. sugar	1/2 c. heavy cream, whipped
1 T. hot strong coffee	semi-sweet chocolate for
	garnish

Melt the white chocolate and the butter over low heat and stir in the nuts. Pour mixture into a 9" pie plate lined with foil and buttered. Spread the mixture evenly around bottom and sides of plate to form a chocolate shell. Refrigerate 2 hours, or until firm. When shell is set, peel off the foil and return to the pie plate. Put the shell back in the refrigerator. Using a blender or food processor, put semi-sweet chocolate, sugar, coffee, egg and yolk in the container and turn on the machine. Add scalded cream and rum and blend for about a minute. Pour the mixture into a bowl and allow to cool. Fold whipped cream into the mixture and spoon it into the shell. Cover and refrigerate 3 or 4 hours, or until filling is set. When ready to serve, remove pie from pan and transfer to a pretty plate. Make chocolate curls with a vegetable peeler and heap them onto the top of the pie.

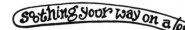

Your own creations...

♥
Apple Centerpiece ♥

To make a whimsical festive centerpiece, use apples and taper candles. Select apples that stand on end well. Core them 3/4 of the way through and place a taper candle in the center of each apple. Place three or four apples down the center of the table and fill in with holly and greenery.

Casserole Cozies

Make a fabric casserole cozy out of a quilted fabric placemat or heavy, finished piece of fabric. Cut out the fabric around the dish and allow an inch or so above the sides for hemming. Fit the corners around the casserole dish by pinching them together and sewing two buttons opposite each other on each of the four corners.

Fabric-Lined Baskets

Baskets are fairly easy to come by, and inexpensive ones can be dressed up with a fabric lining. Select any cheerful fabric appropriate to the season or occasion. Cut it into a circle to fit into the basket and hem the edge. Tack the fabric securely onto the basket around the rim and a few places on the inside. You can also create a fabric basket cover by cutting out a strip of fabric about 12" high and wide enough to fit all the way around the basket. Tack one edge of the fabric to the edges of the basket. Hem the other edge and finish with a drawstring. Makes a good basket warmer for bread and rolls.

Paper Doll Chain

Let your kids help you decorate your tree with memories of childhood...a dolly chain! Take a piece of sturdy paper, about 16 inches long and five inches high. Pleat the paper strip into fanfolds about two inches wide. Fasten pleats together with paper clips at the top and bottom. Draw one-half of a doll silhouette onto your paper. Using sharp scissors, cut out the shape. Make as many chains as desired and tape together. Spray with gold paint, or let the kids color the dolls for you.

Sort through your button box for the smallest of treasures.

Cozy Winter Warmers
welcome recipes for rosy winter cheeks

Cranberry Hot Toddies
Hot Buttered Rum
Jack Frost Warm-up
Hot Jalapeño Poppers
Creamy Crab Bisque
Warm Sweet Potato Muffins
Spicy Rolled Rum Cake

This is the week
when Christmas comes.
Let every pudding
burst with plums,
And every tree bear
dolls and drums,
In the week when
Christmas comes.

– Eleanor Farjeon

Cranberry Hot Toddies

It's sure to warm you to your toes!

16 oz. can jellied cranberry
   sauce
1/3 c. light brown sugar,
   firmly packed
1/4 t. ground cinnamon
1/4 t. ground allspice
1/8 t. ground cloves

1/8 t. ground nutmeg
1/8 t. salt
2 c. water
2 c. unsweetened pineapple
   juice
6 t. butter

Empty cranberry sauce into a large pot. Whisk in sugar and seasonings. Add water and pineapple juice. Cover and allow to simmer for about two hours. Pour into mugs and top each mug with a pat of butter. Serves 6-8.

Hot Buttered Rum

Sometimes grownups need a bit more of a chill-chaser.

- 1 lb. butter, softened
- 2 lb. brown sugar
- 1 1/2 T. ground cinnamon
- 1 qt. + 4 oz. boiling water
- 1/2 t. ground nutmeg
- 1 t. pure vanilla extract
- 1 c. rum
- 6 cinnamon sticks

Mix together butter, brown sugar, cinnamon, nutmeg and vanilla. Add boiling water and a cup of rum (more or less) to the mixture. Pour into 6 mugs and garnish with the cinnamon sticks.

Jack Frost Warm-up

A warm apple drink that goes well with gingerbread!

- 1 qt. apple cider
- 1/4 c. brown sugar, packed
- 5 whole cloves
- 1 cinnamon stick

Heat all ingredients slowly over low heat in a 2-quart saucepan for 20 minutes. Remove cloves and cinnamon stick. Serve warm topped with orange slices or whipped topping and a sprinkle of nutmeg.

Make your favorite hot chocolate extra special. Add a scoop of vanilla ice cream. Then top with whipped cream and dust with cocoa powder. Add a cinnamon stick and sprinkle some chocolate curls on top. Totally yummy!

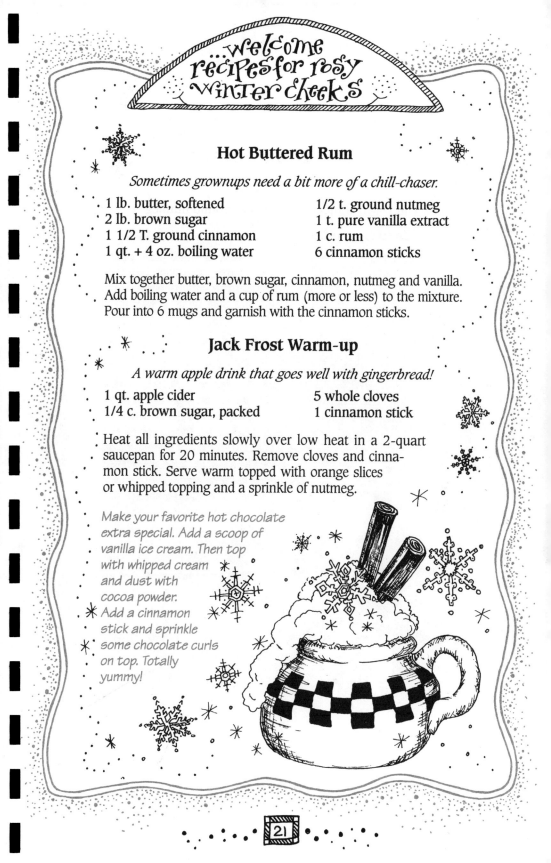

Hot Jalapeño Poppers

A favorite appetizer for those who love a bit of heat.

16 whole preserved jalapeño
  peppers, stemmed and seeded
1 lb. cream cheese, softened

4 T. vegetable oil
1 egg, beaten
1 c. bread crumbs

Open the end of each pepper with a small knife to remove the stem and seeds. With a pastry tube or small sandwich bag with one corner cut off, fill each pepper with the cream cheese. Heat the oil in a large sauté pan over medium heat while you coat the peppers in the egg and bread crumbs. Carefully place the peppers in the pan and sauté until coating is browned and peppers are heated through, turning occasionally. Drain on paper towels. Serves 4.

While the grownups are visiting, set up a holiday activity just for kids. Arrange a cloth around the Christmas tree, complete with big bowls of popcorn and cranberries for stringing. For older kids, have plenty of construction paper, white glue, scissors, glitter, sequins, markers and scraps of fabric for making garlands, snowflakes and ornaments. Be sure to hang on to all those sweet, humble ornaments your children make through the years. They become more precious as time goes by!

Creamy Crab Bisque

This is one of the richest we've tried!

1 c. crab meat, cleaned and
   chopped
1 regular can condensed
   cream of mushroom soup
1 regular can condensed
   cream of asparagus soup

1 c. light cream
1 1/4 c. milk
1/2 t. Worcestershire sauce
1 t. hot pepper sauce

In a heavy saucepan, mix together the crab meat and the soups. Add the remaining ingredients and heat thoroughly. Serve in soup mugs with oyster crackers alongside.

Serve steaming chowder in hollowed-out rounds of sourdough bread. Cut the scooped-out bread into one-inch cubes for croutons. Season to your liking; then brown them by tossing in a lightly oiled, hot skillet.

Warm Sweet Potato Muffins

Set them out with hot drinks and watch them disappear.

1 1/4 c. sugar
1 1/4 c. canned sweet
  potatoes, mashed
1/2 c. butter, softened
2 large eggs, room
  temperature
1 1/2 c. flour
2 t. baking powder

1 t. cinnamon
1/4 t. nutmeg
1/4 t. salt
1 c. milk
1/2 c. raisins, chopped
1/4 c. walnuts, chopped
2 T. sugar and 1/4 t.
  cinnamon, mixed
  together

Line 24 muffin cups with paper liners. Preheat oven to 400 degrees. Beat together sugar, sweet potatoes and butter until smooth. Add eggs and blend well. Sift together flour, baking powder, spices and salt. Add to sweet potato mixture, alternating with the milk, and stirring to blend. Do not overmix. Fold in raisins and nuts. Fill muffin cups 3/4 full and sprinkle each muffin with the sugar and cinnamon mixture. Bake 25 to 30 minutes, or until muffins test done with a toothpick. Serve warm.

Spicy Rolled Rum Cake

Once you've mastered the cake roll, there's no limit to the impressive desserts you can make using this same technique.

3 egg yolks
2 T. water
3 egg whites
2 T. water
single layer spice cake
   mix, sifted
1 c. walnuts, finely chopped

1/2 c. confectioner's sugar,
   sifted
6 oz. cream cheese, softened
1/4 c. butter, softened
1/2 t. pure vanilla extract
1 c. powdered sugar, sifted
2 T. light rum

Beat egg yolks with 2 tablespoons water until thick and lemon-colored. In large mixing bowl, beat egg whites and 2 tablespoons water until peaks form. Fold yolks into whites. Gently fold in cake mix. Spread evenly in a greased 15"x10"x1" pan that has been lined with waxed paper. Sprinkle with walnuts and bake at 375 degrees for 10 to 12 minutes, or until done. Immediately loosen edges of the cake and turn out onto a clean towel that has been sprinkled with confectioner's sugar. Remove waxed paper. Starting with narrow end, roll up cake and towel together. Cool on rack seam side down. To make filling, beat cream cheese, butter and vanilla until fluffy. Add the confectioner's sugar and beat until smooth. Unroll cooled cake and sprinkle with rum. Spread with the cream cheese mixture. Re-roll cake and refrigerate several hours or overnight. Sprinkle with additional confectioner's sugar and walnuts, if desired.
Serves 10.

The smell of buttered toast simply talked to Toad, and with no uncertain voice; talked of warm kitchens, of breakfasts on bright frosty mornings, of cosy parlour firesides on winter evenings, when one's ramble was over and slippered feet were propped on the fender; of the purring of contented cats, and the twitter of sleepy canaries.
- Kenneth Grahame

Merry, bright ideas...

Christmas Card Wreath

What to do with all those holiday greeting cards? Cut a wreath-shaped circle out of corrugated cardboard and cover it with fabric or paint. Use thumbtacks to attach your cards to the wreath. Tie on a big bow and staple some greenery around the edges. Hang your Christmas card wreath on a wall for all to see; keep adding more cards as you receive them!

Button Barrettes

Your daughter's plain barrettes can be dressed up easily for the holidays with treasures from your button box. Just hot glue the buttons onto the barrettes, overlapping to completely cover. Makes a great stocking stuffer for a little girl.

When trimming your holiday tree, use garland or ribbon to divide the tree lengthwise into sections. Each member of the family gets their own section to decorate. Children especially love this tradition, and look forward to decorating their own special section each year.

Snow Fort

If you're lucky enough to enjoy lots of that sparkly white stuff in the winter, remember to take time to play in the snow. Help your kids build a snow fort by packing wet snow into cardboard boxes. Sprinkle the snow with water to form a frozen block, then turn the box upside down to empty. Stack the snow blocks like bricks to build a wall, a fort, or even a castle!

For a colorful snow fort fill a spray bottle with water and a drop of food coloring and decorate the walls of your fort with red, green or blue!

Cake Stencils

Stencil holiday designs onto your chocolate cakes, coffee cakes and brownies with powdered sugar. Just use heavy paper and sharp scissors to cut out a reindeer, star, Santa or tree shape. Or, use your favorite cookie cutter. Sift or shake powdered sugar onto the cake. If you've baked a large sheet cake, you can create a whole Christmas scene with powdered sugar!

Is the paint flaking off of your glass ornaments? Buy glitter, faux jewels or sequins, or use beads from broken costume jewelry to cover the old paint with sparkles and twinkles.

Christmas Cookie Exchange

...all our favorites, the best of the season

Gingerbread Men
French Chocolate Balls
Mexican Sugar Bells
Orange Lace Cookies
Toasted Hazelnut Cookies
Buttery Cinnamon Stars
Jam Thumbprints
Little Cheesecakes
Frosted Butterscotch Cookies
Snowflake Cream Puffs
Black & White Chocolate Bark
Chocolate Mint Brownies

Hang the merry garlands over all the town.
Smell the spicy odors of cookies turning brown!
The mice have come to nibble, they're feeling mighty gay —
But only little children shall have my sweets today!

- Anonymous

Gingerbread Men

These fun fellows are always invited to cookie parties.
Let the kids help dress them!

1 c. shortening	1 c. sugar
1/2 t. salt	1 c. dark molasses
3 t. baking soda	2 eggs, beaten
2 t. ginger	1 t. instant coffee, moistened
2 t. cinnamon	with tap water
1 t. allspice	5 c. all-purpose flour

Cream together first six ingredients. Then add sugar and molasses and continue to beat. Add beaten eggs, coffee, and 3 or 4 of the cups of flour and continue to beat. Then add remaining flour and mix by hand. (Dough will be very stiff.) Cover with plastic wrap and refrigerate overnight or for several hours. Flatten the dough on a floured board and cut out shapes with cookie cutters or mold shapes by hand. Use diced raisins or currents, chocolate chips, sprinkles and candies to dress your gingerbread men. Bake at 325 degrees for about 20 minutes, or until brown.

For unusual gift ribbons, shop your fabric store for remnants. Cut scraps of fabric like gingham, dotted Swiss, flannel or velvet into strips to make unique package ties!

French Chocolate Balls

*So rich, so chocolatey, crunchy on the outside and soft
on the inside...a chocolate-lover's dream!*

2 eggs
1/2 c. + 3 T. sugar
4 oz. unsweetened chocolate,
   grated
1/2 t. cinnamon

1 t. vanilla
5 T. + 1 t. flour
2 c. plus 6 T. almonds, finely
   ground
1 c. powdered sugar, sifted

Beat eggs together with sugar until light and fluffy. Add all remaining ingredients and beat well. Pat dough into a ball and chill 1 hour. Spoon out dough and make into small balls, one inch in diameter or smaller. Roll each ball in the powdered sugar. Allow to dry for several hours at room temperature on a greased baking sheet. Bake at 475 degrees for 4 minutes, or until they've formed a light crust. Allow to cool 10 minutes in the pan; then remove to cooling rack. Makes about 4 dozen.

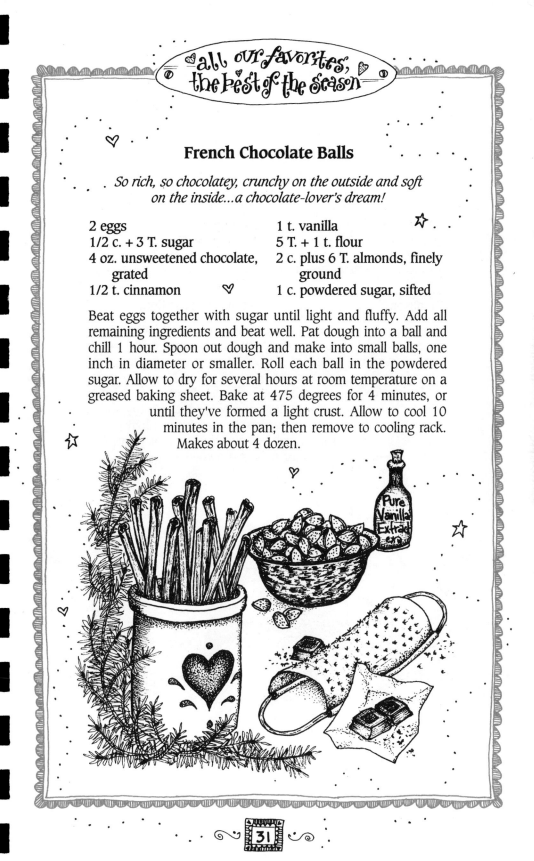

Mexican Sugar Bells

Sweet and tender.

2 c. all-purpose flour
1 c. whole wheat flour
1 t. baking powder
1/2 t. salt
1 c. solid vegetable shortening

3/4 c. sugar, plus more for
   dipping
1 1/2 t. anise seeds
4 to 6 T. cold water

Lightly grease 3 cookies sheets. Sift the flours, baking powder and salt together onto wax paper. Beat the shortening until soft. Add the sugar and anise seeds and beat until light and fluffy. Reduce to lowest speed of mixer and slowly add the sifted flour mixture, beating just until combined. Gradually add the water, using just enough so the dough holds together. Wrap dough in plastic and refrigerate for an hour or so. Roll out the dough onto a lightly floured surface to 3/8" thick. Cut into bell shapes, or any shapes desired. Dip the tops of the cookies in the sugar to lightly coat. Place 1/2" apart on baking sheets and bake at 350 degrees for about 20 minutes, or until lightly browned. After they have cooled, store in an airtight container. Makes about 4 dozen.

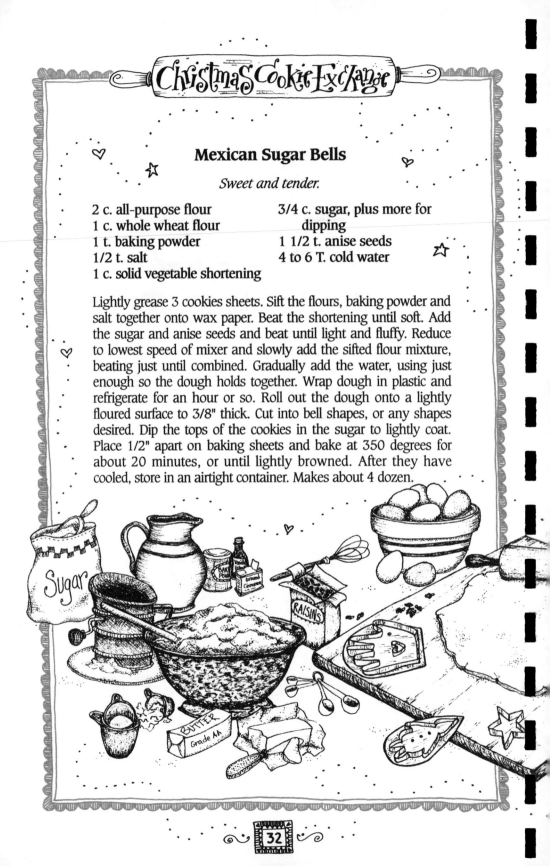

Orange Lace Cookies

*Brown sugar and pecans
combine with orange peel for a chewy crunch.*

1/4 c. unsalted butter, softened
2 c. light brown sugar, packed
2 large eggs, well beaten
1 t. pure vanilla extract
1 t. dark rum
1/2 c. all-purpose flour

1 t. baking powder
2 c. pecans, chopped
1/2 c. candied orange peel
8 oz. semi-sweet chocolate,
melted

Cream butter and sugar with high speed of mixer until fluffy. Add eggs and beat until well blended. Stir in vanilla and rum. In a separate bowl, combine flour and baking powder. Stir in pecans and orange peel. Add this to the butter mixture and combine until just blended. Chill the batter 1 hour. Grease and flour 3 baking sheets. Drop the batter onto the sheets by half-teaspoonfuls, about 3" apart. Bake at 375 degrees about 7 minutes, or until set. Cool 3 minutes; then transfer to cooling rack. When cookies are completely cool, drizzle melted chocolate over the top. Allow chocolate to set before serving. Makes about 8 dozen.

Toasted Hazelnut Cookies

Oh...the warm, toasty flavor of hazelnuts!

3 c. all-purpose flour
2 t. baking powder
1/2 t. salt
11 oz. jar chocolate-hazelnut
   spread*
1/4 c. vegetable shortening
1 1/3 c. sugar

1 t. pure vanilla extract
2 eggs
1/3 c. milk
1/2 c. hazelnuts, chopped
   and toasted
2 c. hazelnuts, finely chopped
3/4 c. powdered sugar, sifted

Stir together flour, baking powder and salt. In a separate bowl, combine chocolate-hazelnut spread and shortening. Beat with electric mixer on medium speed until combined. Add sugar and beat until fluffy. Add vanilla and eggs; beat until combined. Gradually add flour mixture and milk, alternating until combined. Stir in the chopped hazelnuts. Cover and chill 2-3 hours, until firm. Shape dough into 1 1/2" balls. Roll the balls in the finely chopped hazelnuts; then roll in powdered sugar. Place 2" apart on a lightly greased cookie sheet. Bake at 375 degrees for 8 to 10 minutes, or until surface is cracked. Cool on a rack. Makes 5-6 dozen.

*chocolate-hazelnut spread can be found in many groceries and gourmet food shops

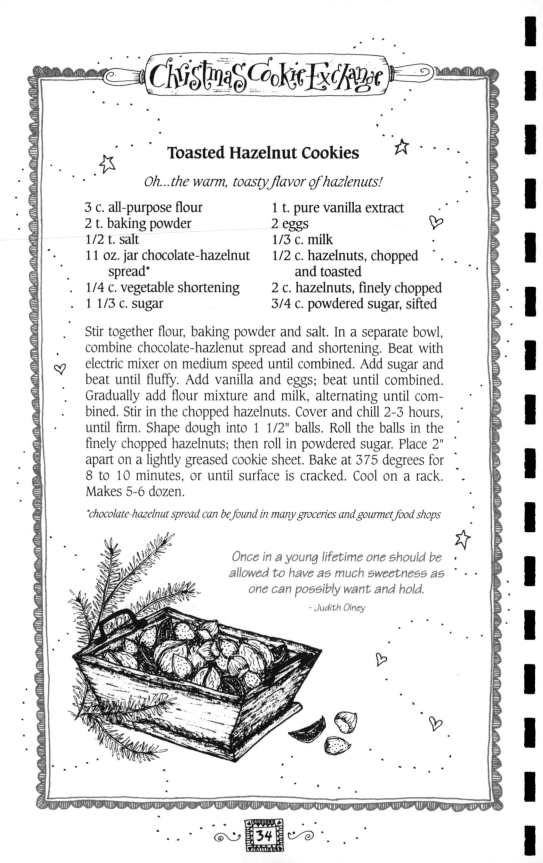

Once in a young lifetime one should be allowed to have as much sweetness as one can possibly want and hold.

- Judith Olney

Buttery Cinnamon Stars

Festive little butter-rum cookies.

1 c. unsalted butter, softened
1 c. sugar
2 1/4 c. almonds, ground fine
1 egg
2 1/2 t. ground cinnamon

zest of one orange, grated
1/4 c. dark rum
3 1/3 c. all-purpose flour
1/2 t. baking powder
1 egg, lightly beaten, for glaze

Cream the butter and sugar. Add the almonds and egg and beat until fluffy. Add the cinnamon and orange zest and rum; beat until smooth. In a separate bowl, stir together the flour and baking powder. Add to the butter mixture and combine lightly. Wrap the dough in plastic and refrigerate about 1 hour, until firm. Roll out the dough on a lightly floured surface to a thickness of 1/4" and cut out stars or other favorite shapes. Place cookies 1/2" apart on greased baking sheet. Brush the cookies with the beaten egg and bake at 350 degrees for about 10 minutes, until light golden in color. After cookies are completely cooled, store them in an airtight container. Makes 6-7 dozen.

Make your own vanilla sugar for flavoring coffees or sprinkling on cookies. Simply put a vanilla bean in a jar of sugar and seal tightly. The longer it sits, the stronger the flavor!

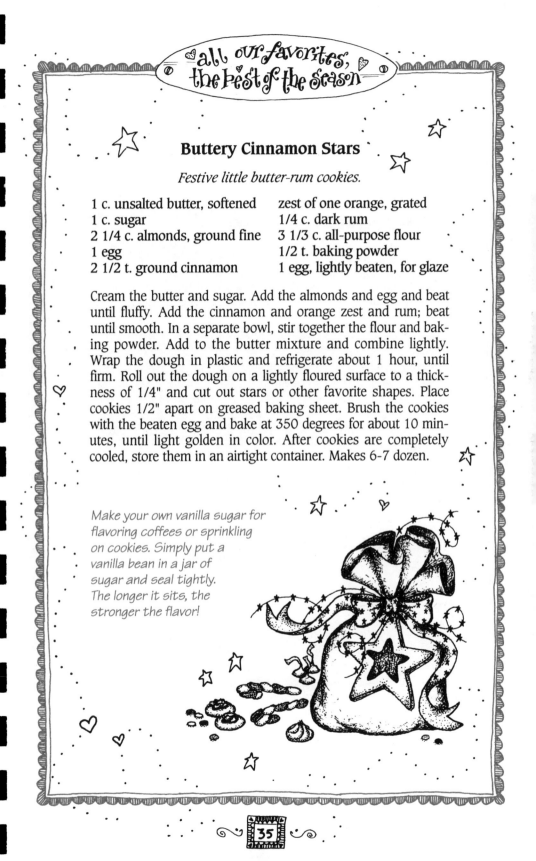

Jam Thumbprints

*Children love to help out by
jamming their thumbs into these cookies.*

3 c. all-purpose flour
1/2 c. sugar
1/2 c. dark brown sugar,
   packed
1 t. ground cloves
1 t. ground cinnamon
3 c. pecans, chopped fine

strawberry, raspberry or
   other favorite jam
1/8 t. salt
2/3 c. unsalted butter, melted
3 large eggs, well beaten
1 t. baking soda
1 T. hot water
2 t. pure vanilla extract

In a large bowl, combine the flour, sugars, cloves, cinnamon, nuts and salt until blended. Stir in the butter and eggs until just combined. Dissolve the baking soda in the hot water and stir into the batter; stir in vanilla. Spoon the dough by teaspoonfuls onto greased baking sheets. Make a thumbprint in the center of each cookie and fill with your favorite jam. Bake at 325 degrees for 10-15 minutes, or until lightly browned on the bottoms. Makes about 3 dozen.

Little Cheesecakes

*Everyone loves these creamy little cakes.
Have fun with different toppings!*

3-8 oz. packages cream cheese
1 c. sugar
5 eggs
1 t. vanilla extract
2 c. sour cream

1/3 c. sugar
1/2 t. vanilla extract
1 can cherry or blueberry pie
   filling for topping

Cream the cheese and sugar together until fluffy. Add eggs and 1 teaspoon vanilla. Bake in paper-lined muffin tins filled 2/3 full at 300 degrees for 40 minutes. Remove from the oven and let stand 5 minutes. Mix together sour cream, 1/3 cup sugar and remaining vanilla and frost the cakes. Return cakes to the oven for 5 minutes; then allow to cool and freeze while still in the muffin tin. When ready to serve, thaw at room temperature for 45 minutes. Top each one with with pie filling. Makes about 20 cakes.

Frosted Butterscotch Cookies

*Get out your favorite cookie cutters
for these decorated delights!*

Cookies:

1 c. butterscotch chips	1/2 c. sugar
1 c. butter, softened	1 egg
3 c. all-purpose flour	2 T. milk
1/2 c. brown sugar, firmly packed	2 t. pure vanilla extract

Melt butterscotch chips in a small saucepan over low heat, stirring constantly. Pour into large mixing bowl; add remaining ingredients. Beat at low speed until well mixed. Divide dough in half and wrap in plastic wrap. Refrigerate 1 hour. Roll out dough on lightly floured surface to 1/8" thickness. Cut into your favorite shapes. Place 1" apart on lightly greased cookie sheets and bake 5 to 8 minutes, or until browned on the edges. Allow to cool before frosting. Makes about 4 dozen.

Frosting:

2 c. confectioner's sugar	2 T. milk
1/4 c. butter, softened	1 t. vanilla

Combine all frosting ingredients and beat at low speed until fluffy. Use food coloring and divide frosting into different colors, depending on how you want to decorate your cookies.

Who says cookie exchanges can only happen at Christmas time? We all tend to get a little isolated in the winter. Spread a little cheer by inviting friends over for a Valentine cookie or dessert exchange in February, when cabin fever really starts to take over!

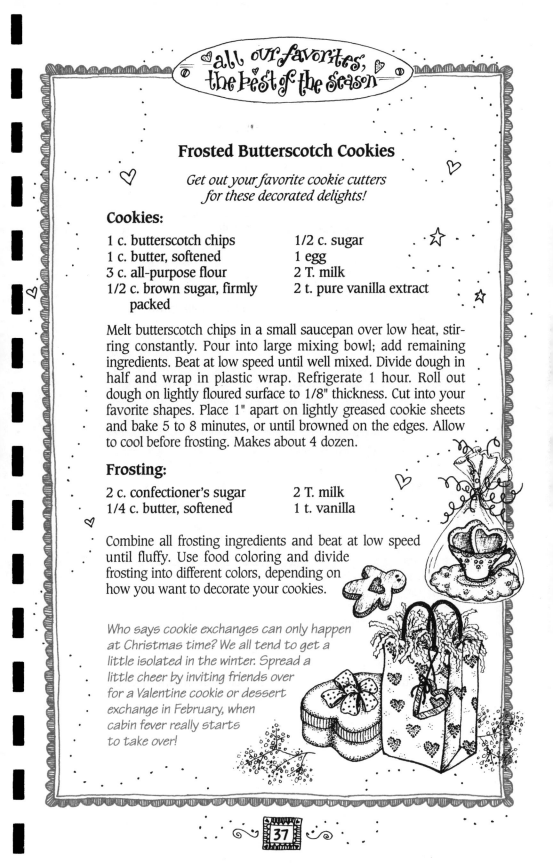

Snowflake Cream Puffs

One of the most coveted treats in the cookie exchange!

1 c. water
1/2 c. butter
1 c. all-purpose flour
4 eggs
1 1/2 c. whipping cream

1/2 c. plus 2 T. powdered
sugar, sifted
powdered sugar to sprinkle
on top

Combine water and butter in a medium saucepan and bring to a boil. Add flour, stirring vigorously over low heat until mixture leaves the sides of the pan and forms a smooth ball. Remove from heat. Add eggs, one at a time, beating until batter is smooth. Pipe the dough into small balls on greased baking sheets, using a decorating tip if desired. Bake at 400 degrees for 20 minutes, or until golden brown and puffy. Allow to cool. Cut the top 1/3 off the cream puffs and set aside; pull out and discard the soft dough inside. Beat whipping cream until foamy; gradually add the powdered sugar, beating until soft peaks form. Fill cream puffs with whipped cream; replace tops of puffs. Sprinkle with powdered sugar. Makes about 3 dozen.

Black & White Chocolate Bark

Rich chocolate flavors magically swirled together.

6 squares semi-sweet baking chocolate
6 squares white baking chocolate
1 c. toasted walnuts, chopped*

Microwave chocolates in separate bowls on high for 1 minute; stir, then microwave another minute, or until almost melted. Stir until completely melted. Stir 1/2 cup of nuts into each bowl. Line a cookie sheet with wax paper. While still warm and runny, alternately spoon the chocolates onto the wax paper. With a butter knife, swirl chocolates together to make a marble pattern. Refrigerate one hour, or until firm. Break into pieces. Makes 1 pound. *To toast walnuts, place in baking pan and toast 7 to 10 minutes at 350 degrees, stirring frequently.*

Chocolate Mint Brownies

Be sure to make plenty; these will not last!

4 squares unsweetened
   chocolate
1/4 lb. plus 4 T. butter
1 c. sugar
2 eggs, beaten
1/2 c. flour

1 c. powdered sugar
cream or milk
peppermint extract to taste
green food coloring to
   desired color

Melt 2 squares of chocolate with a stick of butter. Take from heat, add sugar and mix. Add eggs and mix again. Blend in flour and mix well. Pour into greased 13"x9" pan and bake at 350 degrees for 15 minutes. In a separate bowl, prepare frosting by combining powdered sugar, 2 tablespoons butter, cream (to desired consistency), peppermint extract and green food coloring to taste. Spread frosting on brownies. Refrigerate 1 hour. Melt 2 squares of chocolate with 2 tablespoons butter and drizzle over green frosting. Refrigerate 30 minutes. Cut when firm.

Holly lore: The number of berries on a holly plant is said to forecast winter weather. Few berries means a mild winter, as the birds will be able to find food from many sources. An abundance of berries means extra provisions for the birds in view of a harsh winter ahead.

Christmas Cookie Exchange

Cookie exchanges are even more fun when each guest brings copies of their recipes for sharing. As a special holiday surprise, make a "cookie cookbook," and mail a copy to each guest. What a nice way to remember all of the festivities during a blustery January!

Holiday how-to's...

☆ ### Molded Chocolate Cups

Fill them any way you like! You'll need a cup of semi-sweet chocolate chips and eight paper cupcake liners. Partially melt the chocolate in top of double boiler over hot water. When chocolate is partially melted, remove from heat and let it stand to melt completely. Dip a small brush into the chocolate and paint the inside of the cupcake liners, building up the sides thickly so the cups won't break when paper is removed. Turn onto a baking sheet and refrigerate until hardened. Carefully peel off the paper. Store cups in a cool area. Fill cups with pudding, ice cream, melted chocolate and peanuts, chocolate mousse, whipped cream and crushed cookies or candies.

♡ ### Giant Heart Cookie ♡

Any time of the year that a celebration calls for cookies (birthdays, anniversaries, congratulations), mix up a batch of your favorite chocolate chip cookie dough. Spread the dough into an 8 inch or 9 inch heart-shaped baking pan (dough should cover the bottom of the pan and be about 1/4 inch thick). Bake as usual, being careful to watch closely. Allow to cool slightly and turn your giant cookie out of the pan onto a cooling rack. When completely cool, pipe colorful icing around the edge and write a special message inside.

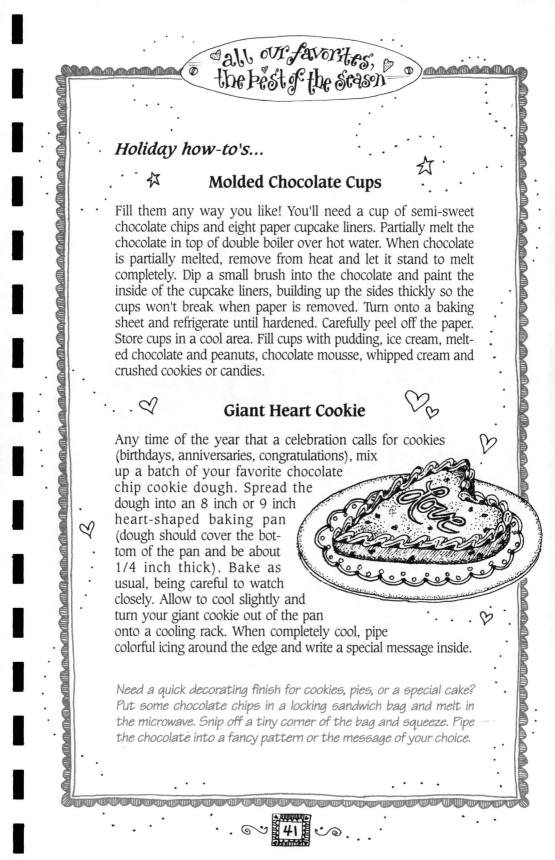

Need a quick decorating finish for cookies, pies, or a special cake? Put some chocolate chips in a locking sandwich bag and melt in the microwave. Snip off a tiny corner of the bag and squeeze. Pipe the chocolate into a fancy pattern or the message of your choice.

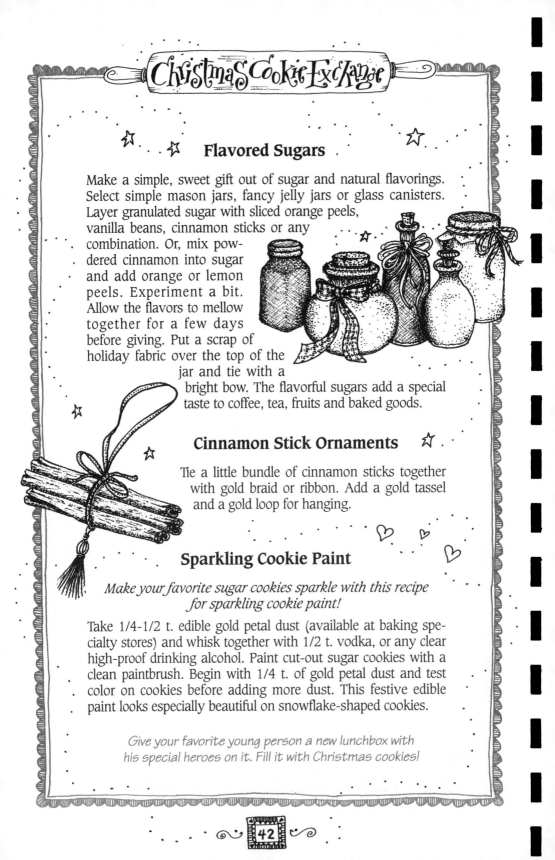

Flavored Sugars

Make a simple, sweet gift out of sugar and natural flavorings. Select simple mason jars, fancy jelly jars or glass canisters. Layer granulated sugar with sliced orange peels, vanilla beans, cinnamon sticks or any combination. Or, mix powdered cinnamon into sugar and add orange or lemon peels. Experiment a bit. Allow the flavors to mellow together for a few days before giving. Put a scrap of holiday fabric over the top of the jar and tie with a bright bow. The flavorful sugars add a special taste to coffee, tea, fruits and baked goods.

Cinnamon Stick Ornaments

Tie a little bundle of cinnamon sticks together with gold braid or ribbon. Add a gold tassel and a gold loop for hanging.

Sparkling Cookie Paint

Make your favorite sugar cookies sparkle with this recipe for sparkling cookie paint!

Take 1/4-1/2 t. edible gold petal dust (available at baking specialty stores) and whisk together with 1/2 t. vodka, or any clear high-proof drinking alcohol. Paint cut-out sugar cookies with a clean paintbrush. Begin with 1/4 t. of gold petal dust and test color on cookies before adding more dust. This festive edible paint looks especially beautiful on snowflake-shaped cookies.

Give your favorite young person a new lunchbox with his special heroes on it. Fill it with Christmas cookies!

Holiday Open House
...a festive buffet for family and friends

Baked Brie with Tomato Sauce
Caraway Breadsticks
Toasted Almonds
Savory Cheese Coins
Sweet 'n Sour Meatballs
Wild Rice Salad
Spicy Crusted Ham
Cranberry-Orange Salsa
Wine-Marinated Beef Brisket
Colorful Christmas Salad
Brandied Peaches
Gingerbread with Crunchy Topping
Hot Rum and Cider Punch
Old-Fashioned Eggnog

There are no bells in all the world
so sweet as sleigh bells over snow.
The horses arch their necks to hear
that pretty music as they go.
If it is dark, you cannot see
the horses curvetting and prancing,
but you would know to hear the bells
that those who shook them
must be dancing.
- Elizabeth Coatsworth

Baked Brie with Tomato Sauce

There's something about this Brie that brings out the fiercest of appetites!

1 frozen pastry shell, thawed	1/2 T. fresh basil, chopped
8 oz. Brie, chilled	1 T. fresh parsley, chopped
1 T. olive oil	1 small bay leaf
1 medium onion, chopped	salt & pepper to taste
2 garlic cloves, crushed	1 T. raisins
13 oz. can tomatoes, drained and chopped	2 T. pine nuts

With a rolling pin, flatten the pastry shell and roll out to a size that will completely cover the cheese. Wrap the cheese in the pastry, tucking the ends in snugly underneath. Make sure there are no openings in the shell. Chill the wrapped cheese for an hour. While cheese is chilling, heat the olive oil in a skillet and sauté the onion and garlic until tender. Stir in the remaining ingredients. Allow to simmer for 15 minutes. Place chilled cheese in a 350 degree oven and bake for 15 minutes, until browned. Spoon tomato sauce into a serving plate and place the cheese on top, discarding the bay leaf. Serve with crackers and caraway breadsticks.

Caraway Breadsticks

The perfect accompaniment to your baked Brie.

16 oz. pkg. hot roll mix   1 large egg, beaten
1 T. caraway seeds   1 T. coarse salt

Prepare hot roll mix, following label directions, through the kneading process. Allow dough to rest 15 minutes while you grease 2 cookie sheets. Divide dough into 24 pieces. On lightly floured surface, roll each piece of dough into an 8" long stick and place on cookie sheet. Cover and let rise in a warm place for about 30 minutes, or until doubled in size. Heat oven as directed on hot roll mix. Brush breadsticks with beaten egg and sprinkle with caraway seeds and salt. Bake 10-15 minutes, or until golden. Serve warm. Makes 24 breadsticks.

Toasted Almonds

For extra flavor, add a bit of garlic salt and paprika!

Spread whole almonds in a single layer in a shallow pan. Place in a cold oven; toast at 350 degrees for 8 to 12 minutes. If you use slivered, chopped, or sliced almonds, toast only 5 to 10 minutes. Keep an eye on them; stir occasionally until lightly toasted. Remove from pan and allow to cool. Serve as an appetizer, or a crunchy addition to salads, desserts and main dishes.

Savory Cheese Coins

These make good prizes for children playing dreidel.

8 oz. sharp cheddar cheese, shredded
1/2 c. butter, softened
1 c. all-purpose unbleached white flour

1 t. Worcestershire sauce
2 T. instant minced onions
pinch of cayenne pepper

Combine all ingredients in a medium bowl and mix well by hand or with a heavy-duty mixer until a dough is formed. Divide the dough in half and shape each half into a log about 1" in diameter and 12" long. If desired, roll in sesame seeds to coat (optional). Wrap the logs in plastic and chill 3 or 4 hours or overnight. When logs are completely chilled, cut each log into about 48 round slices of 1/4" thickness. Place on greased or coated baking sheets and brown in a 375 degree oven for 10 minutes or so. Remove coins from baking sheets to cool. Store in an airtight container. Makes 7 dozen.

Sweet 'n Sour Meatballs

We just had to include this old family favorite!

1 lb. lean ground beef
1 c. soft bread crumbs
1 egg, slightly beaten
2 T. onion, minced
2 T. milk
1 clove garlic, minced

1/2 t. salt
1/8 t. pepper
1 T. vegetable oil
2/3 c. chili sauce
2/3 c. current jelly
1 T. prepared mustard

Combine all ingredients except oil, chili sauce, jelly and mustard. With wet hands, form into 40 bite-size meatballs. Brown meatballs lightly in oil. Cover and cool over low heat for 5 minutes. Drain fat. Combine chili sauce, jelly and mustard and pour over meatballs. Heat, stirring occasionally, until jelly is melted. Simmer at least 15 minutes, until sauce has thickened, gently stirring to combine flavors. Makes 40.

Many's the long night I've dreamed of cheese — toasted, mostly.
- Robert Louis Stevenson

Wild Rice Salad

A hearty, chewy, nutty side dish filled with good vitamins.

2 c. wild rice, cooked
1/2 c. white rice, cooked
1/2 c. diced red bell pepper
1/2 c. chopped tomato
1/4 c. green peas, cooked
1/4 c. red onion, diced
1/4 c. green beans, cooked
   and cut into pieces

4 T. frozen apple juice
   concentrate
2 T. red wine vinegar
2 T. fresh basil, chopped
1 T. fresh parsley, chopped
1 T. fresh tarragon, chopped
1 T. fresh lime juice
salt & pepper to taste

Combine all ingredients in a large bowl, toss well, and season to taste.

Spicy Crusted Ham

The centerpiece of your holiday buffet.

5 lb. whole ham
1 1/3 c. dark brown sugar, packed
3/4 c. soft bread crumbs
2 t. ground mustard
1/2 t. ground cinnamon
1/2 t. black pepper, freshly ground
1/4 t. ground cloves
1/4 c. pineapple juice

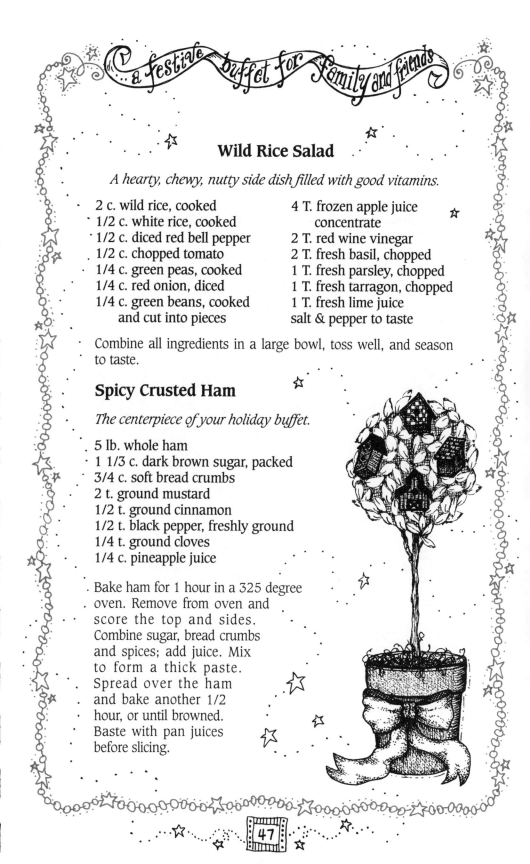

Bake ham for 1 hour in a 325 degree oven. Remove from oven and score the top and sides. Combine sugar, bread crumbs and spices; add juice. Mix to form a thick paste. Spread over the ham and bake another 1/2 hour, or until browned. Baste with pan juices before slicing.

Holiday Open House

Cranberry-Orange Salsa

A little flair from the Southwest.

2 c. dried cranberries
3/4 c. fresh orange juice
1 T. orange zest, minced

2/3 c. toasted pecans
4 t. red chili powder

Puree all the ingredients in a blender or food processor. Serve with ham or turkey.

Oven-Toasted Potato Chips

Thick, rustic chips that brown a bit unevenly for extra crunch.

1 lb. new potatoes, sliced 1/8-inch
thick, skins on

2 T. olive oil
1/2 t. salt

Rinse the sliced potatoes in a colander with very cold water and pat dry. Toss in the oil and half of the salt. Spread in a single layer on a baking sheet. Toast in a preheated 500 degree oven on the top rack for 20-25 minutes, until golden brown. Sprinkle with remaining salt. Serve warm.

Softened cream cheese is perfect for piping into cherry tomatoes and pea pods, or onto celery sticks. Garnish with a dash of paprika.

Wine-Marinated Beef Brisket

*Serve with an assortment of breads
and flavored mustards for sandwiches.*

1 c. dry red wine
2 T. soy sauce
2 garlic cloves, minced
1 celery stalk, thinly sliced

1 small onion, grated
3 to 3 1/2 lb. brisket,
  trimmed of fat
1 medium onion, thinly
  sliced

Mix together the first 5 ingredients and put in a glass baking
dish. Add the brisket and turn over in the marinade so it's completely coated. Cover meat and allow to marinade for several
hours in the refrigerator, turning occasionally. (If your brisket is
still frozen, you can let it thaw while it sits in the marinade.)
Transfer brisket to a large iron skillet and arrange the sliced onion
around it. Pour half the marinade over the meat,
reserving the rest. Cover the pan with aluminum
foil or a tightly-fitting lid and roast at 325 degrees,
basting occasionally, for about 3 hours or until
tender. If the meat seems to be drying out, add
marinade while it cooks. Remove from the oven
and let cool a bit before you slice thinly and
transfer the meat to a serving dish. Pour any
pan juices over the slices. Serves about 8 as a
main dish, or serve cold with sandwich buns
and horseradish.

Colorful Christmas Salad

The one dish children always remember.

3 oz. pkg. lime gelatin
1 c. crushed pineapple, drained
1/2 c. mayonnaise
8 oz. pkg. cream cheese, softened
1/2 c. walnuts, chopped
3 oz. pkg. cranberry gelatin
1/2 c. cranberry sauce

Prepare lime gelatin as directed on package and chill until slightly thickened. Fold in pineapple. Pour into an 8" pan or mold and chill until firm. Add mayonnaise to cheese, mixing until well blended. Add nuts and spread over molded gelatin layer. Chill until firm. Prepare cranberry gelatin and add cranberry sauce. Pour over cheese mixture and chill until firm. Remove from mold by placing mold in hot water for a few minutes; then gently turn onto a serving platter.

Brandied Peaches

Also makes a special gift from your holiday kitchen.

2-29 oz. cans peach halves
3 drops almond extract
1/2 c. peach brandy
1 c. sugar

Drain the peaches, reserving 1 cup of juice. Mix the sugar with the reserved juice and boil until reduced by one-half. Cool this mixture and add the brandy and the almond extract. Pour brandy syrup over the peaches and serve, or pack peaches and brandy syrup into a sterilized one-quart glass jar and seal.

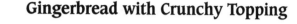
Gingerbread with Crunchy Topping

It can't be Christmas without gingerbread!

1/2 c. vegetable shortening
1/2 c. sugar
1 egg
1 c. molasses
2 1/2 c. cake flour, sifted
1 c. hot water

1 1/2 t. baking soda
1/2 t. salt
1 t. ground ginger
1 t. ground cinnamon
1 t. ground cloves

Cream shortening and sugar with an electric mixer. Add egg and beat well. Add molasses and beat well. Sift together flour, soda, salt, ginger, cinnamon and cloves. With mixer on slow speed, add dry ingredients alternately with the hot water, beating to blend. Pour batter into greased and floured 13"x 9" baking pan. Bake at 350 degrees for 30 minutes; then sprinkle with crunchy topping. Bake 10 minutes longer, or until toothpick comes out clean. Serves 8-10.

Crunchy Topping:

1 c. dark brown sugar, firmly
   packed
1/2 c. flour
1 t. ground cinnamon

1/2 c. butter, cut into pieces
peel of 1 lemon, grated
1 c. pecans or walnuts,
   chopped

Combine sugar, flour, cinnamon and ginger in a bowl. With pastry blender or two knives, cut butter into mixture until it resembles coarse meal. Mix in lemon peel and nuts. Sprinkle mixture over ginger-bread 10 minutes before the end of baking time.

Had I but a penny in the world, thou shouldst have it for gingerbread.
- Shakespeare

Holiday Open House

Hot Rum and Cider Punch

Goes well with gingerbread or pumpkin pie!

1 qt. apple cider	1 qt. light rum
2 T. maple syrup	1 lemon, sliced into 12 slices
2 T. sugar	12 whole cloves
4 oz. fresh lemon juice	12 cinnamon sticks

Heat the cider and stir in syrup and sugar. Add lemon juice and rum; garnish with lemon slices stuck with cloves. Place a cinnamon stick in each cup. Serves 12.

Old-Fashioned Eggnog

When was the last time you had real eggnog?

6 eggs	1 c. golden rum
1 c. sugar	1 qt. light cream
1/2 t. salt	nutmeg

Beat eggs until light and foamy. Add sugar and salt, beating until thick. Stir in rum and cream. Chill several hours. Sprinkle with nutmeg just before serving.

This ancient silver bowl of mine, it tells of good old times,
Of joyous days, and jolly nights, and merry Christmas chimes.
They were a free and jovial race, but honest, brave and true
That dipped their ladle in the punch when this old bowl was new.

— *Oliver Wendell Holmes*

Homespun magic...

Paper Snowflakes

It's fun and easy to make pretty paper snowflakes for hanging in your windows all through the winter. Just take a piece of heavy white paper and cut it into a square with all four sides even. Then fold several times. Use scissors to cut the folded paper into various shapes such as triangles, squares and diamonds. When you unfold the paper, you'll have a beautiful design. Carefully press with a warm iron to remove the creases. Then have fun decorating your snowflakes! Use gold or silver metallic spray paint, or cover with glitter or sequins. Your kids will love coloring them with markers, then adding sparkly glitter with glue. Just punch a hole in the top and they're reading for hanging...in windows, on your mantle, in mirrors, on a large plant, on your Christmas tree, above a doorway...anywhere at all.

Potpourri Ornaments

Here's an easy idea that your friends will enjoy! Pick up some baby-sized woolen mittens or socks from a craft bazaar or baby store. Fill each mitten about 2/3 full with spicy potpourri and tie closed with twine, ribbon or yarn. Give as a tree ornament or a drawer sachet.

Clothespin Angels

Your kids will enjoy helping you make angel ornaments out of clothespins. You'll need wooden clothespins, white acrylic paint, construction paper (pale colors of pink, white, blue and yellow work well) and some scrap sewing notions such as bits of lace, trims and beads. Paint the clothespins white and allow them to dry completely. Glue on sets of construction paper wings and decorate with glitter or sequins and lace. Fashion their faces with tiny beads or fine-point markers. Twist white pipecleaners to make the arms. Use gold metallic ribbons, pipecleaners or rickrack for hair and halos.

Tiny Homemade Stamps

Use miniature metal cookie cutters and artist's gum erasers to make stamps for decorating ribbons and gift wrap. Choose snowflakes, gingerbread men, trees, Santas, leaves or ornaments. Place the eraser on a clean newspaper on the floor, then place the cookie cutter on top of the eraser, put a breadboard or stiff cardboard on top, and step down, using your weight to cut out the stamp. To make a stamp out of the eraser end of a new pencil, take a sharp artist's cutting blade and cut a design out of the eraser. Try cutting out a tiny star or moon shape...or leave it round for polka dots. Dip your tiny stamps into thin pools of acrylic paint or drawing inks, and stamp away!

Candied Orange Stars

4 large oranges
3 c. sugar
3/4 c. water

1/4 c. corn syrup
extra sugar for rolling

A tasty and unusual gift from your kitchen. Remove the skin from the oranges, keeping the peel in quarters, and boil in a large pot of water for a minute. Drain hot water and fill with cold. Boil two more times this way and drain well. Combine sugar, water and corn syrup in another pot and bring to a boil. Add the orange peel and simmer about 45 minutes, or until the peels have absorbed the syrup. Remove peels and cool on a rack. Cut into star shapes with cookie cutters. Roll in sugar and allow to dry completely. Keep in a covered container.

Homemade Holiday Handbags

This time of year, place-mats are plentiful, festive and inexpensive. Fold a fancy fringed tapestry or brocade placemat into an envelope shape. Sew up the sides. Add a button and elastic loop for a fastener. Decorate with ribbon, tassels, pearls, buttons or lace as you wish.

Walnut Jewel Ornaments

Cut a walnut in half and scoop out the nut. With a glue gun, line the inside of the nut with a scrap of fancy fabric, like velvet, satin or brocade. Glue a craft "jewel" to the fabric, in the center of the nut. Outline the outer edge of the naturally heart-shaped nut with little gold beads or tiny pearls. Glue a narrow gold or red fabric bow to the top of the nut, with a loop for hanging.

Make your gift wrapping truly special without spending a penny! Ask your local wallpaper store for discontinued sample books, usually given away. Use the colorful, fun variety of wallpapers to wrap small gifts, or to decorate the larger packages with plaids, stripes, flowers and scenery.

Patchwork Necktie Garland

Old neckties are easy and inexpensive to come by. It seems like the popular width is always changing, and most men toss them out or give them away when they're out of style. Start a collection of clean, but out-of-date ties that you can later use to make a colorful garland. Once you have about 32 ties, cut each one of them about two inches above the point with pinking shears. You can use the pointy ends of the ties to make a garland. Line up the patterns in a colorful sequence and tack them together side to side, patchwork style. Then sew a fancy button or a tassel onto the end of each point. String your "tie garland" across your mantle or over a window or doorway, securing to the wooden sill with a tack or pushpin on each end.

Yuletide Candlelight Dinner

...a joyful Christmas Eve

Baked Artichokes with Mustard Butter Sauce
Prime Rib Roast with Yorkshire Pudding
Creamed Onions with Peanuts
Sour Cream Mashed Potatoes
Glazed Carrots
Pears with Cranberry Relish
Frozen Christmas Salad
Candied Oranges
Walnut Torte
Christmas Wassail
Smiling Bishops

The mistletoe bough on the festive throng
Looks down, amid echoes of mirthful song...
And who is she that will not allow
A kiss claimed under the mistletoe bough?

- English Ballad

Baked Artichokes with Mustard Butter Sauce

*Give yourselves plenty of time
to savor this delectable appetizer!*

6 artichokes (1 per person),
   cleaned and trimmed
1 clove garlic, minced

3 T. olive oil
salt & pepper to taste
seasoned bread crumbs

Sauce:

2 shallots, minced
1 c. dry white wine
1 c. heavy cream

1/2 lb. unsalted butter, softened
2 T. Dijon mustard
salt & pepper to taste

Cut off the stems of the artichokes flush with the bottoms so they'll stand upright. Trim the points off the leaves with scissors. Place in a large pan and cover with cold water. (Place a heavy plate on top of the artichokes so they won't float to the top.) Season the water with the garlic and 1 T. olive oil. Simmer for 40 minutes, or until the leaves pull away easily. Drain and cool. Place in a covered casserole and sprinkle bread crumbs inside the artichokes, pulling the leaves out gently as you go. Drizzle with remaining olive oil. Bake the artichokes, covered, in a 375 degree oven with 1/2" water in the bottom for about 15 minutes. Meanwhile, prepare the sauce by placing the shallots with the wine in a sauté pan. Simmer until wine is reduced by half. Add the cream and simmer until very thick. Whisk in the butter, and season with salt and pepper. When the artichokes are heated through, pour some sauce on individual plates and put an artichoke on each plate. To eat, pull the leaves free with your fingers, dip into the sauce, and scrape the soft white part of the leaf off with your teeth. When you get near the heart of the artichoke, the leaves will be so tender you can eat them whole. Once you have reached the heart, scrape off the white "beard" and eat the tender heart with a fork. Delicious!

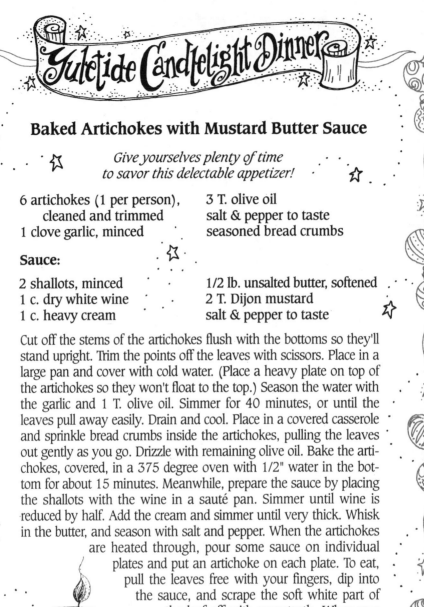

Prime Rib Roast with Yorkshire Pudding

*A glorious roast of prime rib, crusty on the outside,
juicy and pink in the middle, makes the perfect holiday feast.
Yorkshire pudding, steeped in tradition, is an easy recipe that
adds that special touch.*

5 lb. prime beef rib roast
1 c. all-purpose flour, sifted
13 3/4 oz. can beef broth
parsley sprigs

1/2 t. salt
freshly ground pepper to taste
2 large eggs
1 c. milk

Trim roast of fat and place on its rib bones in an open roasting
pan. Sprinkle with pepper to taste. Roast in 325 degree oven
until temperature on a meat thermometer registers 140 degrees
(rare); about 2 hours.

Yorkshire Pudding:

Remove the roast from the oven. In a mixing bowl, whisk eggs
until foamy. Beat in milk and salt. Gradually beat in flour until
mixture is smooth.The last 30 minutes of baking, raise the oven
temperature to 400 degrees, and pour the batter around the
roast. (Keep an eye on the meat thermometer to make sure you
don't overcook the roast!) Cut pudding into squares and arrange
around roast. Garnish with parsley. Serves 8-10.

*"Oh! What a wonderful pudding!"
Bob Cratchit said, and calmly too,
that he regarded it as the greatest
success achieved by Mrs. Cratchit
since their marriage.*
- Charles Dickens, A Christmas Carol

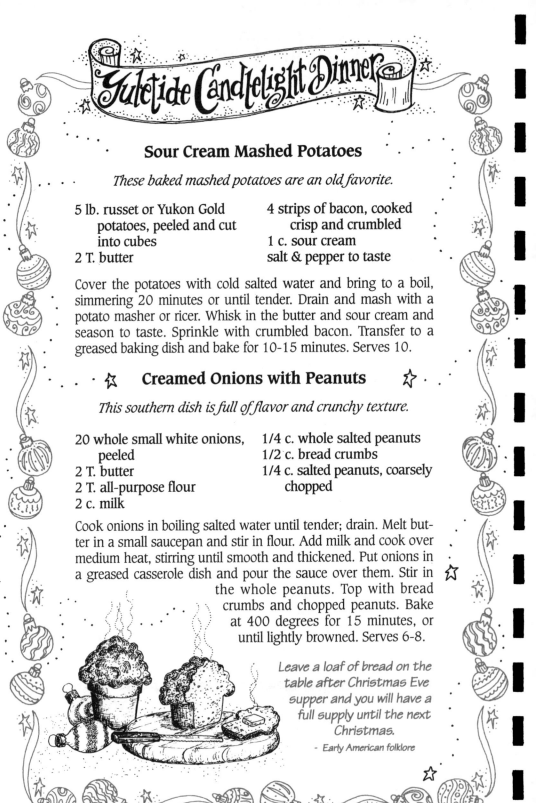

Sour Cream Mashed Potatoes

These baked mashed potatoes are an old favorite.

5 lb. russet or Yukon Gold
  potatoes, peeled and cut
  into cubes
2 T. butter

4 strips of bacon, cooked
  crisp and crumbled
1 c. sour cream
salt & pepper to taste

Cover the potatoes with cold salted water and bring to a boil, simmering 20 minutes or until tender. Drain and mash with a potato masher or ricer. Whisk in the butter and sour cream and season to taste. Sprinkle with crumbled bacon. Transfer to a greased baking dish and bake for 10-15 minutes. Serves 10.

☆ Creamed Onions with Peanuts ☆

This southern dish is full of flavor and crunchy texture.

20 whole small white onions,
  peeled
2 T. butter
2 T. all-purpose flour
2 c. milk

1/4 c. whole salted peanuts
1/2 c. bread crumbs
1/4 c. salted peanuts, coarsely
  chopped

Cook onions in boiling salted water until tender; drain. Melt butter in a small saucepan and stir in flour. Add milk and cook over medium heat, stirring until smooth and thickened. Put onions in a greased casserole dish and pour the sauce over them. Stir in the whole peanuts. Top with bread crumbs and chopped peanuts. Bake at 400 degrees for 15 minutes, or until lightly browned. Serves 6-8.

Leave a loaf of bread on the table after Christmas Eve supper and you will have a full supply until the next Christmas.

- Early American folklore

Glazed Carrots

Carrots add a cheerful, bright splash of color and flavor.

2 T. onion, chopped
2 T. parsley, chopped
2 T. butter
8 carrots, peeled and quartered

10 1/2 oz. can beef
  consommé
1/4 t. sugar

Sauté onion and parsley in butter until tender. Add carrots, consommé, and sugar. Cover and cook 5 minutes. Uncover and cook 10 minutes more, or until carrots are crisp-tender. Sprinkle with a little nutmeg if you like. Serves 8.

Pears with Cranberry Relish

A light, refreshing, healthful medley of fruit colors and flavors.

12 oz. pkg. fresh
  cranberries
2 unpeeled red apples, cored
  and quartered

1 unpeeled lemon, quartered
  and seeded
1 1/2 c. sugar
6 fresh, ripe Bartlett pears

In a food processor, process cranberries, apples and lemon using medium blade until well chopped. Stir in sugar; cover and chill in refrigerator. Cut pears in half lengthwise and hollow out each half with the tip of a spoon. Spoon the relish into the pears and serve. Serves 12.

Frozen Christmas Salad

So cool and creamy!

3/4 bag miniature
    marshmallows
20 oz. can crushed pineapple,
    drained
1/2 c. mayonnaise or salad
    dressing
8 oz. pkg. cream cheese

12 ea. red and green
    maraschino cherries,
    chopped
1/2 c. English walnuts,
    chopped
1 c. whipping cream, whipped

Combine marshmallows and pineapple; set aside until marsh-mallows are well soaked. Mix salad dressing and cream cheese and combine with pineapple mixture. Add chopped cherries and nuts. Whip the whipping cream and fold into the salad. Pour into mold or container of your choice and freeze. Cut and serve on a lettuce leaf. Serves 10.

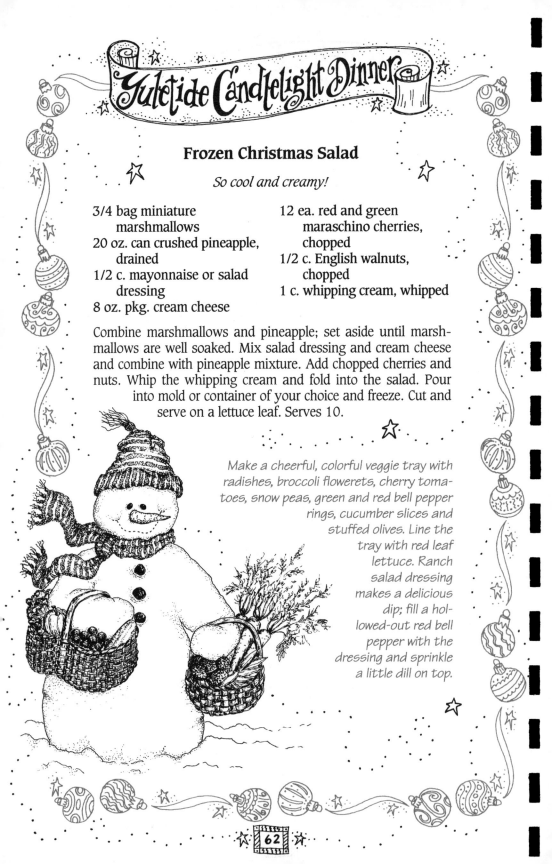

Make a cheerful, colorful veggie tray with radishes, broccoli flowerets, cherry tomatoes, snow peas, green and red bell pepper rings, cucumber slices and stuffed olives. Line the tray with red leaf lettuce. Ranch salad dressing makes a delicious dip; fill a hollowed-out red bell pepper with the dressing and sprinkle a little dill on top.

Candied Oranges

A canister of candied oranges makes a lovely hostess gift.

1 1/3 c. sugar
4 c. water
1T. vanilla
1 t. ground cinnamon
1/2 t. ground nutmeg

6 seedless oranges, skin
   lightly grated to release oils
juice of 1 lemon
1 c. whipped cream
2 T. brandy

Combine sugar, water, vanilla, cinnamon and nutmeg in a large, heavy pot. Bring to a boil, reduce heat to low, cover and simmer for 20 minutes. Add the oranges, making sure they are covered about 3/4 of the way up by the syrup. Cover and slowly cook oranges for 2 hours, turning a few times during cooking. Remove pot from heat and add lemon juice. Place cover back on pot and allow mixture to chill overnight. To serve, slice oranges into wheels and arrange on a pretty plate. Top with whipped cream flavored with brandy.

God bless the master of this house,
Likewise the mistress too;
And all the little children
That round the table go.
- from an English carol

Walnut Torte

A heavenly combination of walnuts with rich coffee and a creamy filling.

8 large eggs, separated	2 T. soft, fresh bread crumbs
3/4 c. + 2 T. sugar	1 T. strongly brewed coffee
1 1/2 c. walnut pieces	2 T. dark rum

Line three 9" round cake pans with wax paper. Then butter and flour the paper. Beat the egg yolks with 3/4 c. of sugar until doubled in volume (about 5 minutes at medium-high with an electric mixer). Set mixture aside. Grind the walnuts with 2 tablespoons sugar in a food processor until very fine. Add walnuts, bread crumbs, coffee and rum to the egg mixture and fold gently. Beat the egg whites just until stiff and fold into the egg yolk mixture. Pour the batter into the cake pans. Bake about 24 minutes, or until lightly golden. The cake should spring back when touched with a fingertip. Allow to cool about 10 minutes; loosen with a knife and place on a rack, removing the paper. When cake is completely cooled, prepare the filling with:

1 1/2 c. heavy cream, well chilled	1 1/2 T. instant coffee powder
	3/4 c. powdered sugar

Stir the coffee into a small amount of the cream until dissolved. Add the remaining cream and the sugar. Beat until cream is very fluffy and forms soft peaks. Spread the whipped cream over each layer and arrange toasted walnuts, or garnish of your choice, on top. Chill 1 hour before serving. Serves 12.

Christmas Wassail

The traditional grog for singing carols 'round the piano.

1 gallon apple cider
1 qt. orange juice
1 c. fresh lemon juice
1 qt. pineapple juice
24 cloves
4 sticks cinnamon
1 c. brown sugar

Mix all ingredients in a large pot and heat to almost boiling. Reduce heat and simmer about 45 minutes. Remove cinnamon and cloves before serving. Makes 1 1/2 gallons.

Smiling Bishops

In the days of Victorian England, this merry mixture would put even Ebeneezer Scrooge into the holiday spirit!

1 bottle port
8 whole cloves
1 bottle red wine
1 orange, sliced

Heat all ingredients until simmering and strain into mugs. Makes 10-12 servings.

An empty coffee can, sprayed with gold paint and tied with a gold ribbon, suddenly becomes a dramatic vase for a bouquet of holly and berries.

Yuletide Candlelight Dinner

Festive little touches...

Fire and Ice Centerpiece

Make pretty candle centerpieces by freezing tall pillar candles in empty milk cartons. Just center the candle in the carton and stuff pine cones and greenery around the candle, enough to hold it upright and keep it centered. Fill the milk carton to just below the top of the candle so the wick stays dry. Freeze solid, then peel paper carton away by dipping briefly in warm water. Set your frozen centerpiece in a cut glass punch bowl or serving tray. Surround it with more pine cones and greenery, and wind some gold or silver florist's ribbon all around. Beautiful!

Painted "Stained Glass" Windows

Did you know you could paint your windows with poster paint? Just mix the paint with a tiny bit of dishwashing liquid. Make up a sketch of your design in miniature, then paint your stained glass design on the inside of a window. Use black paint in a very fine line to outline the shapes clearly. When the sun shines in, your window will be beautiful! Wash it all off with window cleaner when the holidays are over.

Decorating Fun with Paper Doilies

• Take a square doily and fold into an envelope shape, gluing the sides together. Cut heavy card stock (any color you choose) to fit the envelope and use as gift tags, special greeting cards, or placecards for your holiday table.

• Use paper doilies as a liner for cookie platters.

• Glue a scrap of doily to colored paper, fold in half, and use as a gift tag. Secure with a ribbon.

• Use doilies as stencils for sprinkling powdered sugar over cakes and cookies.

• Doilies look beautiful used as linings for bread baskets.

• Use them as gift wrap for small boxes, such as for jewelry.

Decorated Leaves

Leaves can be dipped into gold or silver paint, or sprayed with a light frosting of color. They make beautiful decorations for homemade greeting cards, package tie-ons or garlands. After you've dipped or painted your leaves, tie satin ribbons around the stems and use to dress up gift packages, placecards, or your Christmas tree. Certain leaves have special meanings: Aspen stands for imagination, maple for strength, and birch for good fortune and new beginnings. Make a pin out of a gold-dipped leaf and give it to someone you love.

Yuletide Candlelight Dinner

What does the word "Yuletide" really mean?

Though we often hear the word used synonymously with Christmas, Yuletide was actually a pagan festival of the ancient Vikings. It originated long before Christianity, and was held during winter solstice. The Vikings had a festival to commemorate the "rebirth of the sun," during which they carried out rituals to appease the Sun God before another year began. One ritual was the burning of a very large log. The log had to be kept burning until the festival was over, and it was hoped that the light and heat would please the Sun God enough to ensure the return of summer.

The yule log ritual was later adopted by the Christians, who would venture out on Christmas Eve to search for a massive log to drag home and place on the fire. The log was usually oak or apple, and it was blessed by the owners before burning. The idea was to keep the log burning for the entire twelve days of Christmas.

Most of us no longer burn yule logs today, either because the ritual has become less meaningful or because our fireplaces won't accommodate a log large enough to burn for twelve days. However, the yule log tradition has survived in another, symbolic form...that of the Christmas log cake, or Buche de Nöel. Invented by the French, it's a log-shaped cake covered in chocolate. These delicious gourmet cakes serve as a flavorful reminder of long-ago yuletide seasons.

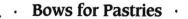

Bows for Pastries

It's so easy to make bows out of gumdrops. Just flatten a handful of large gumdrops with a rolling pin on a pastry board sprinkled with sugar. Make a large square or rectangle; then cut it into strips and form the softened gumdrops into a bow. Use it to top a Christmas cake; "wrap" the cake with ribbons to make a package!

It's an old English custom to wrap tiny treasures in paper and bake them inside the Christmas cake. A bell means a wedding soon, the thimble blesses its owner, the wishbone grants any wish, and the horseshoe means good luck. Be sure to let your guests know about the surprises before they dig in!

Homespun Christmas Ornaments

You can make your own fabric tree ornaments so easily! Just use your favorite cookie cutters...trees, angels, Santas, gingerbread men, stars and reindeer. With a soft pencil, trace around the cutters onto the back side of a folded piece of fabric. Choose fun country fabrics like mini-checks, calicos and bright Christmas plaids. Pin the two sides together and cut out the shapes, then sew all around with a 1/4 inch hem, leaving an inch-wide opening for filling. Turn fabric rightside-out and fill the shape with fiberfill, cotton, or sweet-smelling potpourri. Sew up the opening.

If you like, you can sew all around the outside of your ornament with colorful yarn. Add beads for eyes, sew on a smile, and add buttons and bows. This is a great project to do with the kids. They'll be so proud of their creations!

Christmas Morning

...Easy, fun and festive fare

Vanilla Coffee
Sunrise Punch
Christmas Casserole
Honey Spiced Ham
Cranberry-Orange Chutney
Pumpkin Nut Bread

*I like days
when feathers are snowing,
and all the eaves
have petticoats showing,
and the air is cold,
and the wires are humming,
but you feel all warm...
with Christmas coming!*

- Aileen Fisher

Vanilla Coffee

A rich, mellow wake-up on Christmas day.

1 1/2 c. milk
1 T. sugar
1/2 t. ground cinnamon

3 c. hot, strong brewed coffee
1 1/2 t. pure vanilla extract
whipped topping

Combine milk, sugar and cinnamon in a saucepan and stir well. Cook over medium heat 2 minutes, or until sugar dissolves. Remove from heat; stir in coffee and vanilla. Pour into mugs and garnish with whipped topping. Sprinkle with cinnamon. Serves 4.

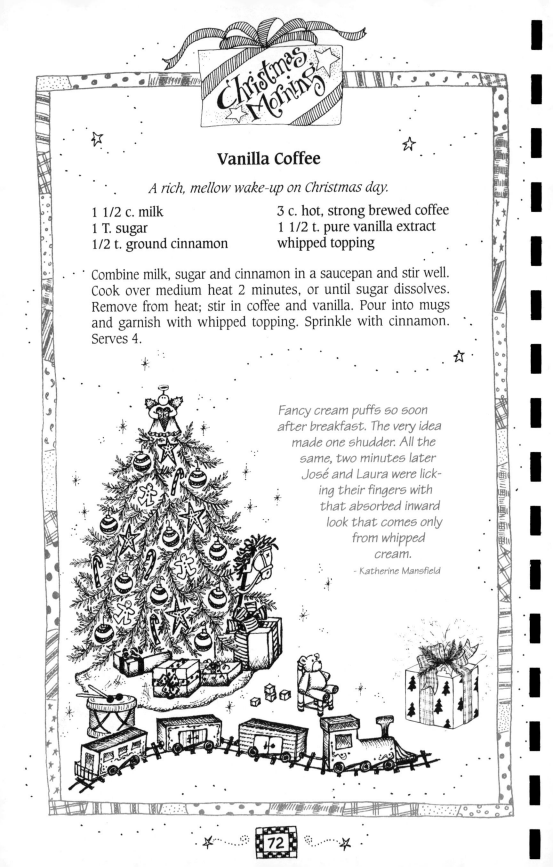

Fancy cream puffs so soon after breakfast. The very idea made one shudder. All the same, two minutes later José and Laura were licking their fingers with that absorbed inward look that comes only from whipped cream.

- Katherine Mansfield

Sunrise Punch

A festive brunch drink for a special occasion.

3 c. unsweetened orange juice
1/2 c. plus 2 T. tequila
  (optional)
1/4 c. fresh lime juice

2 T. powdered sugar
2 T. orange-flavored liqueur
1 T. grenadine syrup
lime slices

Combine all ingredients except grenadine and lime slices in a pitcher and chill. Fill 6 tall glasses with ice and pour in mixture. Slowly add 1/2 teaspoon grenadine down the inside of each glass. Garnish with lime slices.

Christmas Casserole

A Christmas Day favorite;
make it the day before and just pop it in the oven!

5 1/2 oz. seasoned croutons
1 lb. bulk sausage, cooked,
  crumbled and drained
4 eggs
2 c. milk
1 can cream of mushroom
  soup

16 oz. frozen Italian vegetables
1 c. cheddar cheese, shredded
1 c. Monterey Jack cheese,
  shredded

Line the bottom of a 13"x9" baking pan with the croutons. Sprinkle cooked sausage over the croutons. Beat eggs and milk until thoroughly mixed and add remaining ingredients, stirring well. Pour egg mixture over the sausage. Bake at 350 for one hour. Casserole may be prepared ahead and refrigerated before baking. Serves 8.

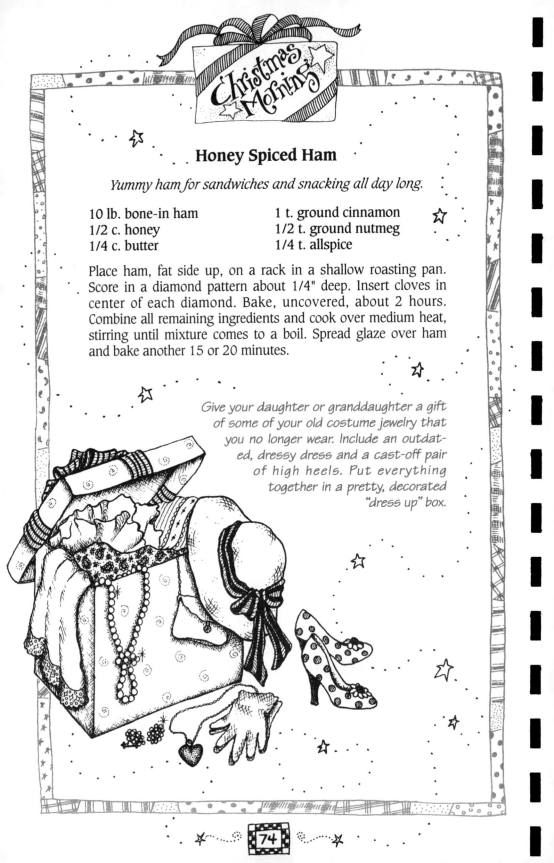

Honey Spiced Ham

Yummy ham for sandwiches and snacking all day long.

10 lb. bone-in ham
1/2 c. honey
1/4 c. butter

1 t. ground cinnamon
1/2 t. ground nutmeg
1/4 t. allspice

Place ham, fat side up, on a rack in a shallow roasting pan. Score in a diamond pattern about 1/4" deep. Insert cloves in center of each diamond. Bake, uncovered, about 2 hours. Combine all remaining ingredients and cook over medium heat, stirring until mixture comes to a boil. Spread glaze over ham and bake another 15 or 20 minutes.

Give your daughter or granddaughter a gift of some of your old costume jewelry that you no longer wear. Include an outdated, dressy dress and a cast-off pair of high heels. Put everything together in a pretty, decorated "dress up" box.

Cranberry-Orange Chutney

An excellent relish for ham sandwiches.

4 seedless oranges
1/2 c. orange juice
1 lb. fresh cranberries
2 c. sugar
1/4 c. crystallized ginger, diced

1/2 t. hot pepper sauce
1 cinnamon stick
1 clove garlic, peeled
3/4 t. curry powder
3/4 c. golden raisins

Peel the oranges and reserve the rind from two of them. Slice the reserved rind very thinly. Cut oranges in 1/4" thick slices and quarter. Combine orange rind with all remaining ingredients and simmer in a saucepan over modern heat, stirring until sugar dissolves and cranberries open. Remove from heat and discard cinnamon and garlic clove. Add oranges and toss lightly. Serve hot or cold with ham. Makes 6 cups.

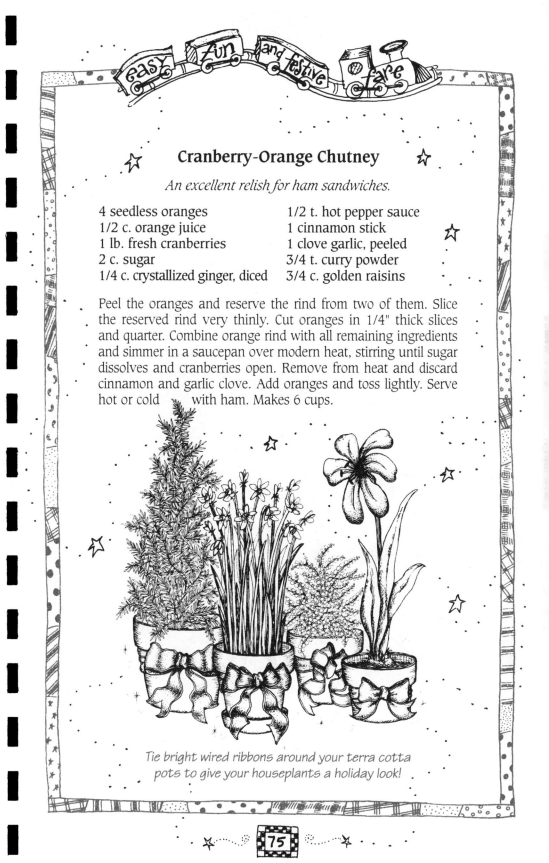

Tie bright wired ribbons around your terra cotta pots to give your houseplants a holiday look!

Pumpkin Nut Bread

Easy snacking for the Christmas crowd.

3 1/4 c. all-purpose flour
3/4 c. quick oats
2 t. baking soda
1 1/2 t. pumpkin pie spice
1/2 t. baking powder
1/2 t. salt
3 eggs

15 oz. can pumpkin
1 1/2 c. sugar
1 1/2 c. packed brown sugar
1/2 c. water
1/2 c. vegetable oil
1/2 c. evaporated milk
1 c. walnuts, chopped

Combine flour, oats, baking soda, pumpkin pie spice, baking powder and salt in a large bowl. Beat together eggs, pumpkin, sugars, water, oil and evaporated milk on medium speed until combined. Beat flour mixture into pumpkin mixture until blended; stir in nuts. Fill 2 greased 9"x5" loaf pans and bake in 350 degree oven for 65-70 minutes, or until toothpick comes out clean. Cool in pans 10 minutes; remove from pans to cool completely.

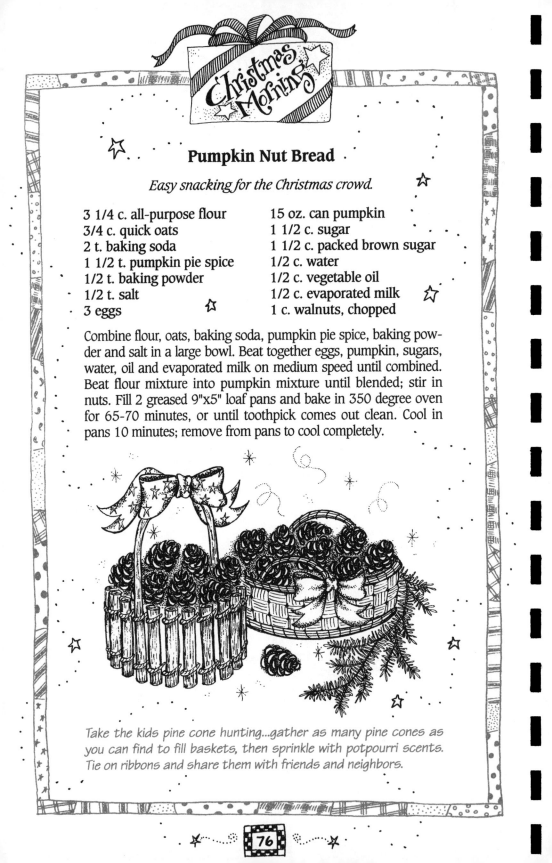

Take the kids pine cone hunting...gather as many pine cones as you can find to fill baskets, then sprinkle with potpourri scents. Tie on ribbons and share them with friends and neighbors.

Keepsakes you can make...

Bay Leaf Votives

Purchase clear glass votive candleholders and white votive candles. Glue fresh glossy bay leaves around the holder with a glue gun. Tie a bow around the middle with gold florist's ribbon. This makes an extra-special placesetting or favor for your guests.

Candle Cups

Shop discount department stores or thrift shops for inexpensive glasses and clear glass mugs. Look for little demitasse mugs, dessert goblets and other interesting shapes. Warm the glasses with hot water; then carefully melt wax and pour into the glasses; add wicks. Experiment with different colors, or add dried rosebuds, straw flowers or clover blossoms to the liquid wax. These special candles make unique gifts...or scatter them about your kitchen and dining area for a warm winter glow!

Little Gold Baskets

Tiny willow baskets, available at most craft and import shops, are just right for painting. A light coat of gold spray paint gives them a sheen, yet allows the woven texture to show through. After they've dried, fill them with foil-wrapped kisses or coins for good luck. Finish with a gold fabric bow, a tiny pine cone and a sprig of greenery. Hang them on the tree; one for each member of your family.

Little girls love to dress up their dolls. Along with that new doll, give her colorful rolls of fabric remnants, along with safety scissors and bits of ribbons and lace, for making doll fashions. The best part of the gift...spend an afternoon helping her invent new styles.

Welcoming the New Year

... around midnight and the day after

Smoked Salmon Canapés
Pimento Deviled Eggs
Patchwork Wheel of Brie
Hoppin' John
Four Cheese and Peppers pizza
Overnight Pork 'n Sauerkraut
Kugel
Monte Cristos
Potato Rivvel Soup Cups
Rich Rum Cake

Ring out the old, ring in the new,
Ring happy bells, across the snow;
The year is going, let him go;
Ring out the false, ring in the true.
- Alfred Lord Tennyson

Smoked Salmon Canapés

For casual gatherings or fancy parties, everyone loves salmon!

1 c. sour cream
1/4 t. lemon zest, finely
   grated
1 loaf of party-sized light rye
   bread, crusts removed

4 T. unsalted butter, melted
1/2 lb. smoked salmon,
   sliced and cut into 1/4"
   strips
2 scallions, thinly sliced

Combine the sour cream and lemon zest and chill for 2 hours. Brush the bread slices with butter and cut each slice in half diagonally. Arrange the bread triangles on baking sheets and bake at 350 degrees for about 10 minutes, or until lightly toasted. Let cool completely. Spoon chilled lemon cream on top of each toast. Place a salmon strip on top and garnish with scallions.

Toasting lore: Back in the sixteenth century, well-wishers used to place a spicy crouton in the wine goblet. The last person to drink from the goblet claimed the "toast," along with good wishes for the future.

Pimento Deviled Eggs

Festive, colorful, and tasty!

1 dozen large eggs, hard-boiled and shelled	1/2 t. ground red pepper
1/4 c. pimentos, chopped	1/4 t. salt
1/4 c. mayonnaise	fresh parsley for garnish
1 1/2 t. Dijon mustard	1/4 red bell pepper, minced

Slice each egg lengthwise in half and remove yolks. Mash yolks with a fork. Stir in pimentos, mayonnaise, mustard, red pepper and salt. Spoon yolk mixture into egg-white halves. (For a more festive look, pipe the yolks into the whites with a star tip.) Refrigerate, covered, until ready to serve. Garnish with fresh parsley and a colorful sprinkling of red bell pepper. Makes 24.

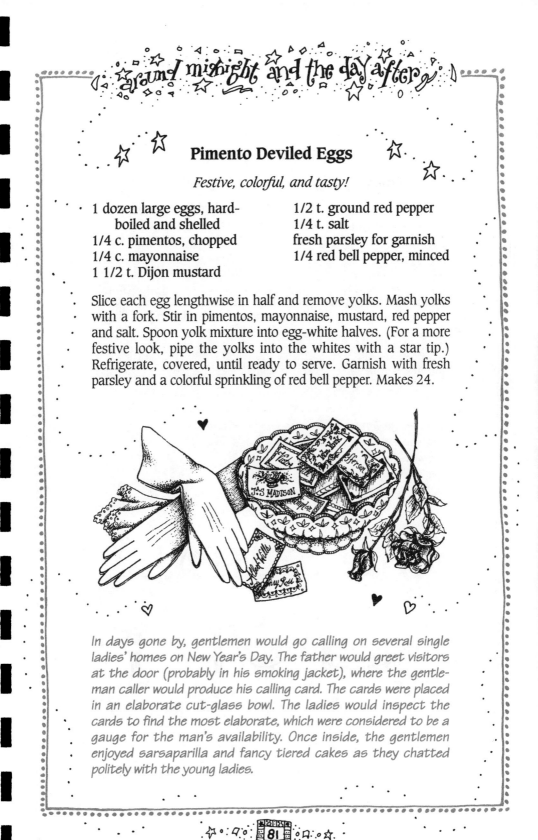

In days gone by, gentlemen would go calling on several single ladies' homes on New Year's Day. The father would greet visitors at the door (probably in his smoking jacket), where the gentleman caller would produce his calling card. The cards were placed in an elaborate cut-glass bowl. The ladies would inspect the cards to find the most elaborate, which were considered to be a gauge for the man's availability. Once inside, the gentlemen enjoyed sarsaparilla and fancy tiered cakes as they chatted politely with the young ladies.

Patchwork Wheel of Brie

A festive centerpiece for your appetizer table.

5 lb. whole, ripe Brie	1 c. fresh dill, chopped
1 c. dried currants	1/2 c. poppy seeds
1 c. walnuts, finely chopped	1 c. blanched almonds, slivered

Remove the rind from the top of the cheese by cutting carefully with a sharp knife. Lightly score the top of the cheese into 10 equal pie-shaped sections. Sprinkle half of each of the toppings onto each wedge and press gently until you have decorated all 10 sections. Allow to stand at room temperature for at least 40 minutes before serving. Serve with water crackers or other light wafers. Serves 20-25.

Long ago in Tennessee, it was the belief that, if you washed your clothes on New Year's Day, you would wash someone out of your family. And, it was considered good luck to eat black-eyed peas!

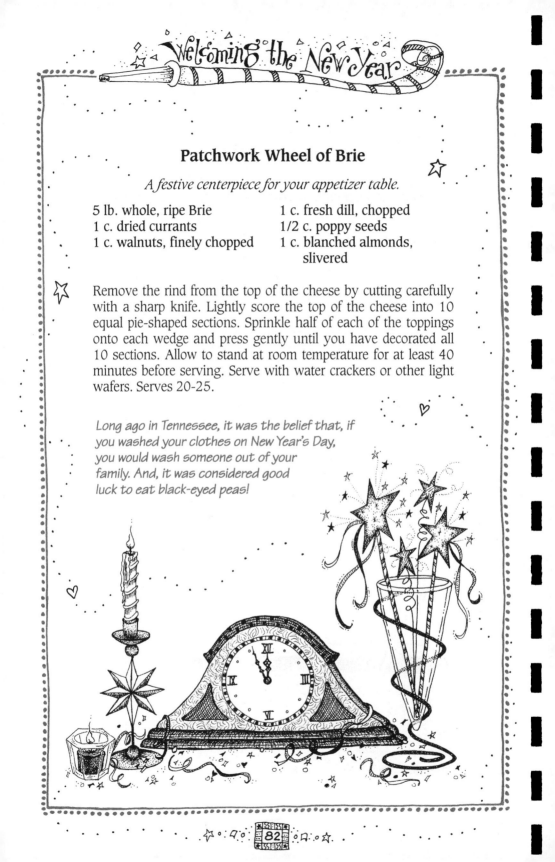

Hoppin' John

Hoppin' John is a traditional good luck stew popular in the South. Eating it on New Year's Day promises a prosperous and healthy New Year.

1 c. black-eyed peas
6 c. water
6 slices bacon, cut up
4 c. water
3/4 c. onion, chopped

1 stalk celery, chopped
1 1/2 t. salt
3/4 t. ground red pepper
1 c. long grain rice

Rinse peas and put in large saucepan with 6 cups water. Bring to a boil and reduce heat to simmer for 2 minutes. Remove from heat, cover and let stand 1 hour. Drain and rinse. In same pan, cook bacon until crisp. Drain off fat, reserving 3 tablespoons. Add peas, 4 cups water, onion, celery, salt and red pepper. Bring to a boil, cover, and reduce heat. Simmer 30 minutes. Add uncooked rice; cover and simmer 20 minutes longer until peas and rice are tender.

In Louisiana, it's good luck to wear something new on New Year's Day. In North Carolina, folklore has it that rice and peas will bring you luck. You'll also have paper money all year if you eat your collard greens! In Maryland, it was tradition to have a masquerade party. All the guests would remain in masquerade until midnight, when they'd reveal their faces.

Four-Cheese and Peppers Pizza

Just double or triple this recipe if you have a crowd of well-wishers!

16 oz. loaf frozen bread
   dough, thawed
1 green & 1 red bell pepper,
   chopped
1 c. mozzarella cheese, shredded
3/4 c. fontina cheese, shredded
1/2 c. Parmesan cheese,
   grated

2 cloves garlic, minced
1/2 c. feta cheese, crumbled
2 t. dried parsley
3 plum tomatoes, thinly
   sliced
1 T. olive oil

Press bread dough into a greased 12" pizza pan. Prick generously with a fork. Bake in a 375 degree oven for 20-25 minutes, until light brown. Top with peppers, cheeses, garlic, spices and tomatoes; brush olive oil over the top. Bake in 375 degree oven for 15-20 minutes, or until cheese is melted. Let stand for a few minutes before cutting. Makes 6 servings.

Use tiny pretzel sticks instead of toothpicks for spearing cheese cubes.

Overnight Pork 'n Sauerkraut

Traditionally, eating pork and sauerkraut on New Year's Day will bring you good luck. Put this casserole in the oven in the wee small hours of the morning, and it'll be ready for you on New Year's Day!

2 lb. lean pork loin, cubed
    into 1" pieces
2 lb. sauerkraut

2 c. onions, sliced
6 slices bacon, cut in half
3 c. water

Brown pork in a large skillet and set aside. Place 1 pound of sauerkraut in a 2-quart casserole dish. Cover with 1 cup onion and the pork. Top with the remaining onions and sauerkraut. Top with bacon. Pour water over the layers and bake, uncovered, at 300 degrees overnight, or about 7-8 hours.

Kugel

A very soothing noodle "pudding"!

8 oz. medium egg noodles
4 T. vegetable oil
4 large eggs
1/3 c. sugar
1 c. orange juice

1/4 t. cinnamon
1/8 t. ground ginger
1/8 t. ground ginger
1 large apple, peeled and
    diced
pinch of salt

Cook noodles according to package directions; drain and toss with 2 tablespoons oil. In a large bowl, mix eggs, sugar, and remaining oil. Add apples. Combine mixture with noodles and transfer to a greased 10" square casserole. Cover and bake at 350 degrees for 40 minutes. Remove cover and bake for an additional 10-20 minutes. Cut into squares and serve.

A bit of German folklore...if you keep herring or cabbage in the house on New Year's Eve, you'll have money all year. If you eat a piece of herring as the clock strikes midnight, you'll be lucky all year.

Monte Cristos

*A hearty breakfast sandwich for those
after-midnight munchies.*

1/4 lb. butter	8 oz. cheddar cheese, grated
8 thin bread slices, crusts removed	4 eggs
	salt & pepper to taste
4 large, thin slices ham	4 slices sweet onion

On a large griddle, melt half the butter and fry four slices of bread until brown. Remove from griddle and place uncooked side of bread down. Place a ham slice and 1/4 of the cheese on each piece of bread. Place the other slice of bread on top of each stack, with the browned side down. Beat the egg with a little salt and pepper and coat the outside of the sandwich with it. Melt the remaining butter in the frying pan, fry the sandwich on each side until golden, and slice each sandwich in half diagonally. Serve immediately; makes 8 wedges.

Early American folklore says that the lady of the house would open first the front door, and then the back door, letting the cold air flow through the house. After a moment she would say, "letting out the old and letting in the new!"

Potato Rivvel Soup Cups

A cup of this hearty soup will warm the coldest New Year!

1 medium onion, chopped	1/2 c. flour
5 potatoes, diced	1/2 c. butter
salt & pepper to taste	1/8 t. celery seed
2 eggs, beaten	1 to 1 1/2 qt. milk
1 t. salt	parsley

Cook onion, potatoes, salt and pepper in boiling water until potatoes are soft. Add salt and flour to the beaten eggs and stir until mixture is lumpy. Add more flour if necessary. Drop the egg rivvels into the potato mixture and boil for 15 minutes. Add butter, celery seed, milk, and parsley and heat thoroughly.

Laugh and be merry together, like brothers akin,
Guesting awhile in the room of a beautiful inn.
Glad till the dancing stops, and the lilt of the music ends.
Laugh till the game is played; and be you merry my friends.

- John Masefield

Rich Rum Cake

There can be no holiday without a delicious rum cake.

4 eggs, separated
1/2 c. brown sugar
1 c. flour
1 t. baking powder
1/4 t. salt
1/3 c. butter, melted
1t. pure vanilla extract

Beat egg whites until stiff and add 4 tablespoons sugar. Beat yolks with remaining sugar and add to egg white mixture. Fold in flour, baking powder and salt and add butter and vanilla. Pour into a greased and floured tube pan and bake at 375 degrees for 25-30 minutes. Remove from the oven and poke holes in the top with a long wooden skewer.

Rum Sauce:

1/4 c. butter
1 c. orange juice
1/2 c. powdered sugar
1/2 c. rum

Melt butter in a small saucepan. Add juice and sugar; stir until sugar is dissolved. Add rum and heat through. Drizzle sauce over cake. Garnish with chopped nuts or fresh orange slices.

Life begets life. Energy creates energy. It is by spending oneself that one becomes rich.
- Sarah Bernhardt

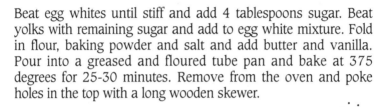

Your own special way...

Ornament Centerpiece

Fill a large, round glass bowl such as a salad bowl, punch bowl or trifle bowl, heaping full of shiny, bright gold and silver ornaments. Wind little white fairy lights around and through the arrangement. Use clear glass plates and gold napkins to complete a festive look for your table. Reflects candlelight and makes a glowing centerpiece...perfect for New Year's Eve!

Christmas Tree Bird Feeder

When you're finished with your tree, prop it up outside and decorate it with food for the birds. Fill the crevices of pine cones with peanut butter, and fill grapefruit or orange rinds with birdseed. Tie to the branches with string. The birds will "decorate" your tree before you know it!

If you've strung your Christmas tree with popcorn, be sure to hang the garlands outside for the birds after the tree comes down! (Make sure the garland has no leftover hooks or tinsel hanging around.)

Wine Glass Wisdom

There are so many interesting glasses available for wines and champagne. Which shape and size suits which type of wine? Champagne is best served in a "flute," or tall, narrow column shape. This helps preserve the bubbles, and allows for best enjoyment of the bouquet. A rounded, apple-shaped goblet is recommended for white wines, and the larger, more generously-sized glasses are for red. The smaller, four to six-ounce glasses are reserved for sherry, port, and madeira as well as the sweeter dessert wines. Though wines can be served in any glasses you choose, these guidelines were established for optimum enjoyment of the wine's flavor and bouquet.

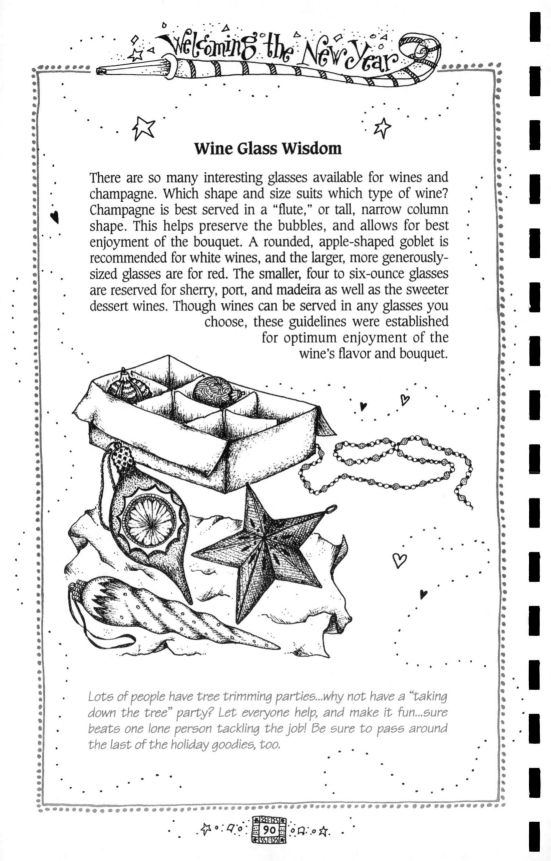

Lots of people have tree trimming parties...why not have a "taking down the tree" party? Let everyone help, and make it fun...sure beats one lone person tackling the job! Be sure to pass around the last of the holiday goodies, too.

Italian Feast

...hearty tastes for cold, blustery days

Roasted Garlic Spread on Italian Bread
Caponata (Sicilian Eggplant Relish)
Bruschetta with Tomato Topping
Pasta with Prosciutto and Kale
Seafood Fettucini Alfredo
Chicken Cacciatore
Sauteed Spinach in Lemon-Garlic Sauce
Beef Bragiole (Stuffed Flank Steak)
Vanilla Spongecake with Cannoli Cream
Tiramisu
Pignoli (Italian Almond Cookies)

We may live without poetry, music and art;
We may live without conscience
and live without heart;
We may live without friends;
We may live without books;
But civilized man cannot live without cooks.

- Owen Meredith

Roasted Garlic Spread on Italian Bread

The roasted garlic has a sweet, nutty taste.

1 medium head of garlic per person
2 t. olive oil per head

additional olive oil for dipping
1 loaf of Italian bread

Peel the dry outer layers of skin from the garlic heads, but leave clove skins intact. Cut off the top, pointed part of the heads so that the individual cloves are exposed. Place in a baking dish and drizzle with olive oil. Bake, covered, in a 400 degree oven for about 30 minutes, until cloves are soft. To serve, offer a cruet of olive oil to be drizzled onto individual bread plates. Each diner can press the soft garlic from the cloves and spread on the bread; dipping their bread into the olive oil.

A wrapped loaf of homemade Italian bread tied to a wooden cutting board makes a heartwarming wintertime gift!

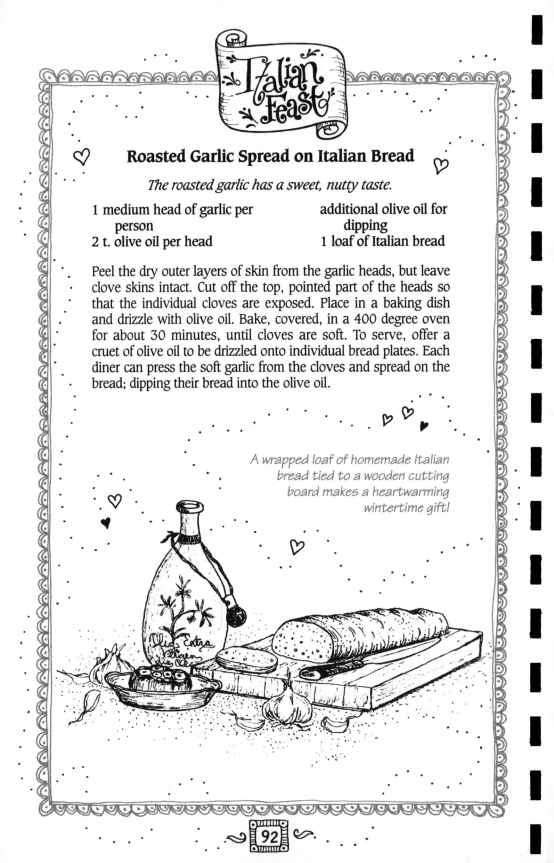

Caponata (Sicilian Eggplant Relish)

This rich, savory relish will keep for weeks in your refrigerator, if there's any left over!

2 medium eggplants, sliced
   and then diced
1/2 c. olive oil
2 large onions, sliced
1 c. celery
16 oz. can tomatoes, strained
   and chopped

2 T. sugar
4 T. vinegar
salt and pepper to taste
1/4 c. green (salad) olives,
   chopped
capers to taste

Slice eggplant and squeeze dry with paper towels. Dice into one-inch cubes. Brown in hot oil 10 minutes, until soft and brown. During last 3 minutes of browning, add onions. Then add tomatoes and celery and simmer for 15 minutes. Add vinegar, sugar, salt and pepper, olives and capers. Simmer 20 minutes longer over low heat. Tastes best when served at room temperature on crackers or crusty Italian bread.

Bruschetta with Tomato Topping

Bruschetta makes an excellent appetizer, and goes perfectly with soup or salad.

8 oz. loaf French bread (baguette) with sesame seeds

2 medium ripe red tomatoes, chopped

1 T. olive oil

1/8 t. pepper

2 T. olive oil

1/3 c. green onion, thinly sliced

1 T. dried basil or oregano, crushed

1/2 c. Parmesan cheese, freshly grated

Cut bread into 1/2" thick slices and brush both sides lightly with olive oil. Place in a single layer on an ungreased baking sheet. Bake in a 425 degree oven about 5 minutes, or until crisp and light brown, turning once. Combine all remaining ingredients except cheese to make tomato topping. Spread each slice with tomato topping and sprinkle with cheese. Bake 2 to 3 minutes longer, or until cheese melts.

Open my heart, and you will see engraved inside of it, "Italy."

- Robert Browning

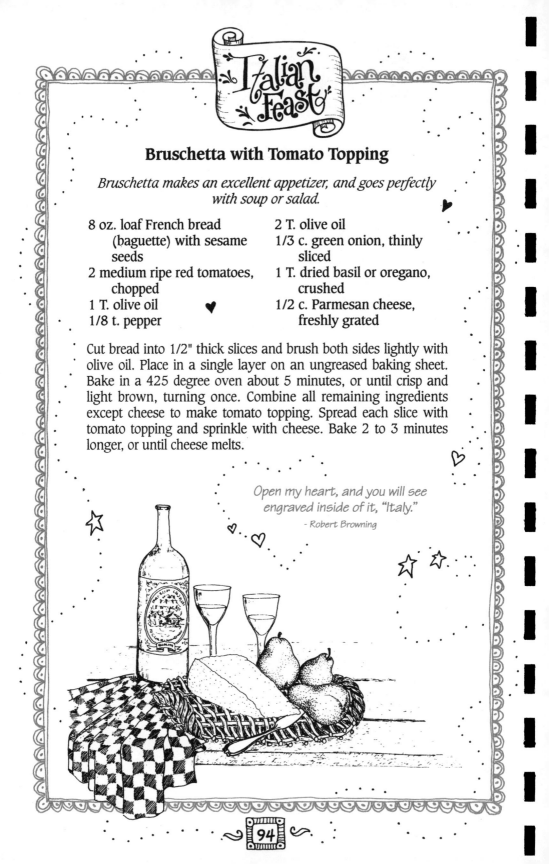

Pasta with Prosciutto and Kale

Italian ham and flavorful kale combine for a hearty taste.

2 lbs. kale, washed, stems
   trimmed off and leaves
   chopped
olive oil to cover bottom of
   pan
6 cloves garlic
1/2 t. red pepper, crushed
1/2 c. parsley, chopped
2 stalks celery, chopped

1/2 lb. prosciutto, chopped
2-28 oz. cans Italian plum
   tomatoes
13 oz. can beef stock
1/2 t. freshly ground black
   pepper
1 t. basil, crushed
1 lb. pasta of your choice,
   cooked al dente

Heat a large pot of salted water to boiling and cook kale stems until tender; then add kale leaves and cook until tender. At the same time, heat olive oil in a large skillet over very low heat. Sauté prosciutto, garlic and celery until soft. Then add broth and tomatoes and cook for about 25 minutes. When kale is very tender, remove from water with a slotted spoon and add to the sauce. Allow to simmer while you cook the pasta of your choice. Serves 6 to 8.

Seafood Fettucini Alfredo

Serve with a tossed green salad and crusty bruschetta for a satisfying dinner.

1/2 c. butter	1 c. half and half
1 lb. fresh crabmeat	1 c. Parmesan cheese, freshly
1 t. green onions, minced	grated
1/2 t. garlic, minced	2 t. fresh parsley, minced
9 oz. pkg. fettucini, cooked	1/2 t. salt
al dente and drained	1/4 t. freshly ground black
	pepper

Melt butter in a large, heavy saucepan and sauté crabmeat, onions and garlic over low heat for 3 to 4 minutes. Remove from heat and stir cooked fettucini into mixture. In a separate container, beat egg yolks, half and half and Parmesan cheese. Add this to the fettucini mixture, toss gently, and cook over moderate heat a few minutes, until sauce thickens. Add parsley, salt and pepper. Serves 4 to 6. Note: This dish also may be prepared with a combination of fresh cleaned shrimp and crabmeat, or with a pound of fresh shrimp.

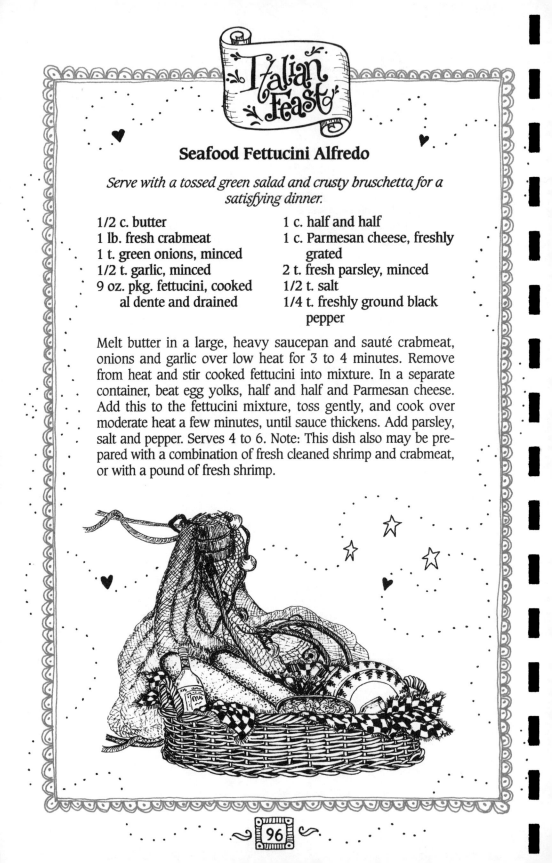

Chicken Cacciatore

A very satisfying dish that's remarkably low in fat!

2 fresh chicken breasts, 2 thighs and 2 legs, skinned
1/4 c. flour
1/2 t. salt
4 T. olive oil
1 onion, sliced
2 cloves garlic, minced
1/2 lb. mushrooms, sliced
16 oz. can Italian plum tomatoes, drained and chopped (reserve juice)
8 oz. can tomato sauce
8 oz. can chicken broth
1 t. fresh or 1/2 t. dried parsley, chopped
pepper to taste
1/2 t. oregano
1/2 t. basil
1/4 c. dry red wine
1/4 c. ripe olives, sliced (optional)
Parmesan or Romano cheese, freshly grated

Dredge chicken in flour and, in a large skillet or Dutch oven, brown in the olive oil until golden. Remove chicken from pan and sauté onion, garlic and mushrooms. Stir in tomatoes, sauce, broth, seasonings, olives, wine, and 1/4 cup reserved juice. Cook a few minutes to blend. Return chicken to skillet; cover and simmer 45 minutes, or until chicken is very tender. Remove bones from chicken, chop chicken and return to pot. Serve over hot cooked spaghetti and sprinkle with cheese.

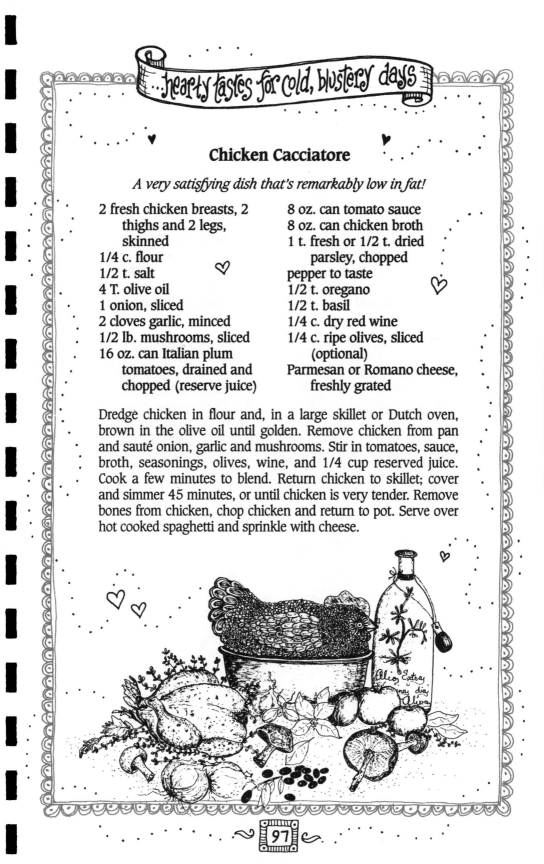

Sautéed Spinach in Lemon-Garlic Sauce

If you don't like spinach, you haven't tasted this dish.

2 T. olive oil
2 cloves garlic, crushed
salt and pepper to taste
1/4 t. red pepper, crushed
    (optional)

1/2 lb. fresh spinach, washed
    and chopped
1 T. fresh lemon juice
1 t. water

Heat olive oil in a large skillet over medium heat. Smash the unpeeled garlic cloves with a large, flat blade and remove skins, mincing any large pieces. Add crushed garlic to skillet and sauté until golden. Add spinach and stir gently. Season to taste. Add lemon juice and water to skillet, cover, and turn heat to low. Allow spinach to wilt for about 3 minutes. Remove lid and stir again. Serve garnished with fresh lemon slices.

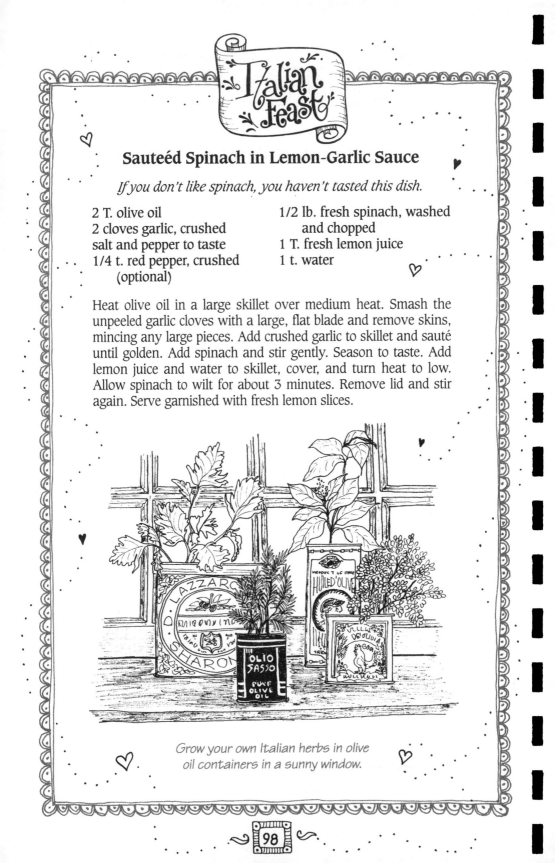

*Grow your own Italian herbs in olive
oil containers in a sunny window.*

Beef Bragiole (Stuffed Flank Steak)

This classic Italian dish is sliced into pinwheels for a festive presentation!

3/4 c. Parmesan or Romano cheese, freshly grated
1/2 c. dried bread crumbs
1 c. green onions, minced
1/4 c. fresh parsley, minced
1/2 lb. fresh spinach, chopped fine (optional)

2 lb. flank steak, tenderized
1/4 c. + 1 T. olive oil
1/4 lb. mushrooms, chopped
1 small onion, sliced
1 T. Worcestershire sauce
1 c. beef broth

Mix together cheese, bread crumbs, green onions, parsley, spinach, garlic, olive oil and mushrooms. Pat mixture on top of the flank steak. Carefully roll up the steak like a jelly roll and tie with cotton twine in 2 or 3 places so roll is secure. Rub meat with Worcestershire sauce. Sear meat until brown in a large skillet with 1 tablespoon olive oil. Place meat in roasting pan with the beef broth and the sliced onion. Cover pan and roast at 300 degrees for about an hour, or until fork-tender. Remove from pan and allow to stand for 10 minutes before slicing. Slice about an inch thick per serving. Serves 4-5.

Italian balsamic vinegar adds a rich, savory taste to many types of dishes. Try sprinkling some on roast chicken or beef, pork chops, brown rice, or a mixed green salad. Marinate chicken in a mixture of balsamic vinegar, garlic and olive oil before baking.

Vanilla Spongecake with Cannoli Cream

Italian spongecake is an excellent base for a variety of cakes, tortes and trifles. Try different fruit and cream fillings such as raspberry, cherry, and vanilla cream.

Spongecake:

4 large eggs, separated
pinch of salt
1/4 c. sugar

1 t. pure vanilla extract
1/4 c. sifted all-purpose flour
1/4 c. cornstarch, sifted
together with the flour

Preheat the oven to 375 degrees and adjust rack to center of the oven. Lightly butter and flour an 8" or 9" springform pan. Beat the egg whites with salt until they form soft peaks. Gradually add the sugar while beating until the whites are just stiff. Do not overbeat. In a separate bowl, whisk the egg yolks and vanilla until blended. Fold in 1/4 of the egg white mixture. Then pour the egg yolk mixture into the whites and sprinkle the flour mixture through a sieve over the egg mixture. Fold flour into the egg mixture thoroughly, but do not overmix. Spread the batter evenly in the prepared pan with a rubber spatula. Bake 25 to 30 minutes, until the cake is golden brown. Allow to cool in the pan for 5 minutes; then turn cake onto a rack and carefully remove the sides of the pan. Allow to cool completely before cutting.

Cannoli Cream:

The orange zest gives this filling a flavor you can't resist.

1 lb. ricotta cheese
2 T. milk or cream
1/3 c. sugar

1 1/2 t. pure vanilla extract
zest of 1/2 orange, grated
2 T. Amaretto or Frangelico
liqueur (optional)

In a blender or food processor, blend the ricotta cheese by pulsing briefly, continuing to pulse until nearly smooth. (Gradually add milk or cream if it seems too dry.) Add sugar and vanilla and continue to blend the cheese until it is smooth and satiny. Add the orange zest and the liqueur. Place a generous dollop on top of each slice of spongecake.

Tiramisu ("Pick-me-up")

*No wonder this fabulous dessert is popular in many
Italian restaurants!*

Use recipe on the previous page for spongecake to make this
delicious dessert.

2 c. milk	1/4 c. light rum
3/4 c. sugar	2 t. pure vanilla extract
6 egg yolks	3/4 c. marscapone (Italian
1/4 c. all-purpose flour	specialty) cheese
1/2 stick unsalted butter, cut	2 c. espresso or very strong,
into pieces	freshly brewed coffee
3 T. semi-sweet cocoa powder	Garnish: Chocolate curls

In a heavy saucepan over medium heat, scald all but 2 tablespoons of the milk together with the sugar. Cook and stir until
the sugar has dissolved completely. In a bowl, beat the egg
yolks with the reserved 2 tablespoons of milk and the flour.
Gradually pour the yolk mixture into the saucepan with the
milk, whisking constantly. Cook over medium heat, continuing
to whisk. Bring mixture to a boil and allow it to boil for two
minutes, still continuing to stir. Remove from the heat and
strain into a clean bowl. Whisk in the butter, rum and vanilla.
Cover the custard with plastic wrap touching the surface and
refrigerate 2 hours. Empty the marscapone cheese into a bowl
and gently fold a few times with a rubber spatula. Gradually fold
in the cooled custard. After spongecake has been removed from
the pan and has completely cooled, cut it horizontally into three
layers with a serrated knife. Put the bottom layer in a springform pan and drizzle with 1/3 of the espresso until it is soaked.
Then spread a layer of custard over the bottom layer. Repeat
this process for the second layer. For the third layer, invert and
moisten with espresso; then turn it browned side up. Spread the
top with the remaining custard. Sift cocoa over the top of the
cake. Refrigerate for one hour. Garnish with chocolate curls.

*A pretty lace or woolen fringed shawl
makes a cozy tablecloth for two.*

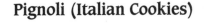

Pignoli (Italian Cookies)

This crunchy little cookie is perfect alongside a dish of spumoni ice cream or a cup of cappuccino.

1 lb. almond paste
1 1/4 c. sugar

4 egg whites
3 1/2 c. pine nuts or almonds, depending on your preference

Break the almond paste into pieces and place in a mixing bowl with the sugar. Use a mixer to crumble the paste and sugar until evenly combined. In a separate bowl, beat the egg whites to soft peaks. Gradually fold the egg whites into the almond mixture. Place the nuts in a shallow bowl. Roll the dough into 1" balls and press each ball into the nuts, gently turning to coat evenly. Place on a buttered baking sheet, spaced about 1" apart. Bake 15 minutes or so in a preheated, 350 degree oven, until light golden in color. Allow to cool 5 minutes on the pan before transferring to a rack. Store in an airtight container.

Fun things to try...

Pasta Necklace

Here's a fun twist on jewelry for kids. Take any hollow pasta shapes, like rigatoni, cannelloni, ditali, macaroni, manicotti, penne or ziti. For color variations, look for spinach pasta as well as wheat pasta. Thread a length of yarn through a large-eye needle, then thread the pasta shapes of your choice. Add some big wooden beads in bright colors. Finish your necklace by knotting the ends together.

Coconut Snowballs

Make a quick party dessert by rolling frozen scoops of ice cream in mounds of shredded coconut. Add crushed nuts or sprinkles if you wish. Experiment with different flavors of ice cream. Serve your snowballs on a chilled platter with chocolate sauce on the side.

Blossoming Branches

You can get winter branches to blossom before springtime...just bring the branches inside where it's warmer, and give them plenty of water. Take a winter walk in the woods, or even in your own back yard, and snip a few branches of apple, cherry, forsythia, huckleberry, dogwood, pear or weeping willow. Just cut the ends on a slant and keep in a container with plenty of water, in a cool spot...below 60 degrees is best. You may want to keep your branches in an enclosed porch, and be sure to mist them occasionally. Be patient; it usually takes three or four weeks before the buds open into flowers.

The Story of Befana, the Good Christmas Witch

The story of Befana begins long ago, with the birth of Christ. It is an old Italian legend that Befana refused to help the three Wise Men when they asked her for directions to Bethlehem. Later, Befana regretted her stubborness and set out to find them. Since Befana never found the Wise Men, she has continued to wander the world.

This benevolent witch carries a big, heavy bag over her shoulder. It's filled with candy and gifts for "good" children and lumps of coal for the "naughty" ones. (Has your mother or grandmother ever warned you that you'd get a lump of coal for Christmas if you weren't good?)

Befana carries a large silver bell that she rings to announce her arrival at each child's house. Maybe she'll come to your house this year!

Nothing but Chocolate

...rich, creamy satisfaction for the most compelling craving

Chocolate Mousse
Chocolate Orange Cake
Frosty Chocolate Pecan Pie
Sweet Chocolate Chunk Cookies
Chocolate Cookie Kisses
Chocolate Bavarian Cream
White Chocolate Mousse Pastries
White Chocolate Chip Macadamia Nut Brownie Pie
Creme de Menthe Sheet Cake
Vanilla Ice Cream with Hot Fudge Sauce

*A house is not beautiful because of its walls,
but because of its cakes.*
- Old Russian Proverb

Chocolate Mousse

Silky smooth and creamy.

6 oz. semi-sweet chocolate
1/2 c. unsalted butter
3 eggs, separated

2 T. sugar
3/4 c. heavy cream
1/2 t. pure vanilla extract

In a double boiler, melt the chocolate with the butter over simmering water. Pour into a bowl and allow to cool to room temperature. Add yolks to chocolate and stir well. In a separate mixing bowl, beat the egg whites to soft peaks. Add the sugar while beating. Whisk a little bit of the egg white into the chocolate mixture; then gently fold in the rest. Whip the cream and vanilla together until stiff; then gently fold into the chocolate mixture. Spoon into serving dishes and chill.

> Spread melted chocolate generously on one side of a sugar cookie. Stick another cookie on top to make a sandwich. You can melt the chocolate squares or chips in the microwave or a double boiler. Put your sandwich cookies in the fridge to set for a few minutes...then decorate!

Chocolate Orange Cake

Citrusy flavor combines with chocolate for an irresistible treat!

1/2 c. + 2 T. unsalted butter,
    divided
1 c. sugar
4 eggs, separated
1 c. all-purpose flour
12 oz. pkg. semi-sweet
    chocolate chips, melted

1/4 c. + 2 T. orange liqueur,
    divided
2 c. powdered sugar
2 oz. white chocolate, melted

Grease and flour a 9" springform pan. Beat together 1/2 cup butter and sugar on high setting of mixer. Add egg yolks. Beat in flour and stir in melted chocolate. Add 1/4 cup liqueur. Beat egg whites until stiff. Stir in 1 cup of the whites into the flour mixture; then fold in remaining whites. Spread batter into the pan and bake at 350 degrees for 45 minutes, or until done when tested with a toothpick. Cool at least 15 minutes; then remove cake from pan. Make frosting by combining powdered sugar, melted white chocolate, orange juice and 2 table-spoons liqueur. Spread over cake. Chill and garnish with orange slices and grated chocolate curls.

Chocolate curls are elegant for garnishing cakes, desserts or hot chocolate. Here's how: Soften white or semi-sweet chocolate by microwaving repeatedly for 8 seconds, or until soft. Use a sharp vegetable peeler and, peeling toward you, make the curls. Or, melt chocolate into a flat baking pan and use a small, flat metal spatula to scrape up large curls. The chocolate must be just the right temperature...too cool, and it will flake; too warm and it won't curl. Practice, practice, practice...don't worry; you can eat your mistakes!

Frosty Chocolate Pecan Pie

This frozen concoction is delightfully rich and crunchy.

Crust:

2 c. pecans, finely chopped and toasted

5 T. brown sugar, firmly packed

5 T. butter, cut into small pieces

2 t. dark rum

Blend all ingredients and press into bottom and sides of a 9" pie plate. Freeze for 1 hour.

Filling:

6 oz. semi-sweet chocolate

1/2 t. instant coffee

4 eggs, room temperature

1 T. dark rum

1 t. pure vanilla extract

1 1/2 c. whipping cream

3 T. semi-sweet chocolate shavings

Melt chocolate with the coffee in the top of a double boiler over hot water. Remove from heat and whisk in eggs, rum and vanilla until mixture is smooth. Allow to cool about 5 minutes. Whip 1 cup of cream until stiff. Gently fold whipped cream into chocolate mixture until blended completely. Pour into prepared crust, cover and freeze. One hour before serving, transfer pie to refrigerator. Whip remaining cream and pipe on top of pie filling. Garnish with chocolate shavings.

Sweet Chocolate Chunk Cookies

America's favorite cookie, now with big, chewy chunks.

3 c. all-purpose flour
1 1/2 t. baking soda
1 1/2 t. salt
1 1/2 c. butter
1 1/2 c. sugar
3/4 c. brown sugar, firmly
    packed

3 eggs
3 t. vanilla
12 oz. sweet cooking
    chocolate, chopped into
    chunks
1 1/2 c. walnuts, chopped

Mix flour with soda and salt. In a separate bowl, cream butter. Beat in sugar, egg and vanilla until light and fluffy. Blend in flour mixture. Add chocolate and nuts and chill for about an hour. For each cookie, measure 1/4 c. dough on an ungreased baking sheet and flatten slightly. Bake 4 or 5 at a time on one sheet at 375 degrees for 12-14 minutes, or until lightly browned. Cool a minute or two before removing from sheet. Makes 36 big cookies.

Chocolate Cookie Kisses

Try creating these elegant chocolate confections with a white chocolate topping, too.

2 large egg whites
1 c. sugar
6 t. unsweetened cocoa,
    sifted

1 1/2 c. toasted almonds,
    medium-fine ground
4 oz. semi-sweet chocolate,
    melted

Beat egg whites on high speed of an electric mixer, until stiff. Then add the sugar and continue beating until egg whites are very thick, 2 to 3 minutes. Beat in cocoa, stir in almonds, and blend completely. Line a baking sheet with waxed paper. With damp hands, shape heaping teaspoonfuls of dough into 1" balls. Form into a "kiss" shape and place on baking sheet about 2" apart. Bake at 325 degrees about 15 minutes, or until cookies begin to crack slightly. Allow to cool 10 minutes; then transfer to a rack. Dip the tip of each cooled kiss into the melted chocolate and allow to harden.

Chocolate Bavarian Cream

Rich, smooth and satisfying.

1 envelope unflavored gelatin	1 c. milk
4 egg yolks	1 c. whipping cream
dash of salt	1 t. vanilla
1/2 c. sugar	2 oz. unsweetened choco- late, melted

Soften gelatin in 1/4 cup cold water and set aside. Mix egg yolks, salt and sugar in the top of a double boiler. Blend in milk gradually, cooking over hot water and stirring constantly until mixture is thick and smooth. Stir in melted chocolate. Add gelatin and stir until dissolved. Allow to cool. Whip the cream, add vanilla, and fold into cooled mixture. Spoon into a one-quart mold and chill.

White Chocolate Mousse Pastries

Ready-made pastry shells are the secret to this easy, elegant dessert!

10 oz. pkg. frozen puff pastry shells	6 squares white chocolate
1 1/2 c. whipping cream, divided	1 square semi-sweet choco- late, melted

Follow directions on pastry shell package and let shells cool. Put white chocolate and 1/4 cup of the whipping cream in a microwave container and cook 2 minutes on high, until chocolate is almost melted. Stir until completely melted. Cool until chocolate reaches room temperature, stirring occasionally. Beat remaining cream in a chilled bowl with electric mixer until soft peaks form. Fold one-half of the whipped cream into the white chocolate; then fold in the other half just until blended. Spoon into the pastry shells. Drizzle melted semi-sweet chocolate over the top. Chill overnight. Serves 6.

White Chocolate Chip Macadamia Nut Brownie Pie

The crunchy macadamia nuts combine with the creamy white chocolate to create a fabulous taste sensation.

1 stick unsalted butter, softened
1 c. sugar
2 eggs
1/2 c. flour

1/4 c. unsweetened cocoa
1 t. pure vanilla extract
1/2 c. macadamia nuts, chopped
3 oz. white chocolate chips

Cream butter and sugar together and beat in the eggs. Add flour, cocoa and vanilla. Fold in the nuts and chips. Pour into a greased 9" pie pan. Bake at 325 degrees for 35 minutes. (Pie should be moist; toothpick will not come out completely clean.) Let cool, but serve slightly warm, if possible, with a scoop of vanilla ice cream on the side.

I don't think a really good pie can be made without a dozen or so children peeking over your shoulder as you stoop to look in at it every little while.

- John Gould

Creme de Menthe Sheet Cake

This cool mint cake makes an excellent holiday dessert.

Cake:

1 c. sugar	1 c. flour
1 stick butter, softened	12 oz. chocolate syrup
4 eggs	

Frosting:

2 1/2 c. powdered sugar	3 oz. creme de menthe
1 stick butter, softened	liqueur
1 T. milk	12 oz. semi-sweet chocolate
	chips, melted

Beat together sugar and butter and add eggs, flour, and syrup. Pour into a greased and floured 13"x9" baking pan and bake at 350 degrees for 25-30 minutes. While cake is cooling, make frosting by combining remaining ingredients, adjusting sugar or milk for desired consistency. Beat with a mixer, and frost the cooled cake. Sprinkle with crushed peppermint candies or chocolate sprinkles.

Hot Fudge Sauce

Keep an extra jar in the fridge for late-night snacks!

1/2 c. unsweetened	1 1/2 c. sugar
cocoa	1 t. vanilla
1 c. sour cream	extract

Using a double boiler, stir all ingredients together and cook for about an hour, stirring occasionally. Drizzle over vanilla or coffee ice cream. Makes 1 pint.

rich creamy satisfaction for the most compelling craving

Aren't you clever...

Chocolate Cake Topper

To make a chocolate disk cake topper, melt white or milk chocolate over a double boiler and stir until smooth. Pour chocolate out onto a waxed paper-lined cookie sheet. Allow chocolate to set slightly, then invert a small bowl on top of it. Using the bowl as a guide, cut around the edge of the bowl with an icing spreader and you'll have a perfect circle. Freeze. Remove chocolate disk from the freezer and, using an icing tip or a plastic bag with a tiny corner cut off, pipe on your greeting with melted white or dark chocolate. Freeze until set. Place disk in the center of your iced cake and serve.

♥ Chocolate Garnishes

Garnish your sheet cakes with chocolate cut-outs or fancy chocolate leaves. It's easier than you think! To make the cut-outs, pour melted milk chocolate onto a waxed paper-lined cookie sheet. Allow chocolate to set slightly at room temperature. Using your favorite mini cookie cutter shapes, cut out the chocolate and remove with a thin metal spatula, placing them again on the waxed paper-lined sheet. Chill in the freezer until firm. To create chocolate leaves, paint the vein side of a nontoxic leaf with melted chocolate. Place leaves in the refrigerator until set; then gently peel off the leaf.

Nothing but Chocolate

Different types of chocolate and their uses

Melting chocolate - Perfect for dipping strawberries and making your own homemade candies. For a real chocolate fix (or quick, thoughtful gift) dip double cream chocolate sandwich cookies (store-bought) into melted milk or dark chocolate. Let set, then drizzle with melted white chocolate.

Semi-sweet chocolate - Pure chocolate perfection. Available in chunks or chips, semi-sweet chocolate has less sugar content and is just right for making chocolate chip cookies or muffins.

Dark chocolate - Pure chocolate with a smooth, rich flavor, not quite as sweet as milk chocolate. Use either dark or milk chocolate in candy-making and baking, depending on your personal preference.

Milk chocolate - Pure chocolate mixed with extra cocoa butter and sugar. Sweet, smooth, and a favorite for snackers.

Cocoa powder - Available in both sweetened and unsweetened varieties. Use for baking cakes, brownies, making frostings and hot chocolate. Extra bonus: cocoa powder is naturally low in fat and cholesterol-free. A good low-fat alternative to baking with chocolate is to replace each square of baking chocolate with 3 level tablespoons of cocoa plus one tablespoon of vegetable oil. For an extra special treat, try sprinkling sweetened cocoa powder on top of vanilla ice cream or yogurt. Yum!

Swiss COCOA

Hearts Afire

...romantic fireside picnic for two

Broiled Oysters
Buttery Squash Soup
Tempting Caesar Salad
Roasted Cornish Hens
Filet Mignon Steaks Flambé
Roasted Baby Red Potatoes
Chocolate Puffs

*The supreme happiness of life
is the conviction that we are loved.*
- Victor Hugo

Broiled Oysters

An oyster is a delicacy we encourage you to try at least once!

1/4 c. butter
1/2 c. bread crumbs
1 T. Parmesan cheese, freshly grated
1 T. dry white wine

1/4 t. dried oregano, crushed
1 garlic clove, crushed
6 oysters on the half shell
paprika to taste
fresh lemon slices

Preheat broiler. Melt butter in small saucepan over medium heat. Stir in bread crumbs, cheese, wine, oregano and garlic and mix well. Spread over oysters while still in the shell. Place on baking sheet and broil for 5 minutes. Sprinkle with paprika and garnish with fresh lemon. Serves 2.

Buttery Squash Soup

Rich, smooth soup to stir the appetite!

10 oz. pkg. frozen cooked squash
15 oz. can chicken broth
1 T. brown sugar, firmly packed

1 T. butter
1/4 c. sliced almonds, toasted

Thaw squash in a microwave oven for 3 minutes on high. Combine squash and broth in a medium saucepan and bring to a simmer over medium-high heat. Allow to gently simmer for 3 or 4 minutes. Add brown sugar and butter and stir until melted. Sprinkle toasted almonds on top. Serves 2.

He was a bold man that first ate an oyster.
- Dean Swift

Tempting Caesar Salad

A crisp, green classic.

2 anchovy fillets
2/3 c. extra virgin olive oil
3 T. fresh lemon juice
1/2 t. freshly ground black
   pepper
1/4 t. salt
1 t. wine vinegar

1 egg
1/2 large head romaine
   lettuce, torn into pieces
1/3 c. Parmesan cheese,
   freshly grated
1 c. croutons

In wooden salad bowl, mash anchovies. Add olive oil, lemon juice, salt, pepper, and vinegar and mix well. Whisk egg into the mixture. Add lettuce and toss well. Sprinkle with cheese and croutons. Serves 2.

Croutons:

3 T. olive oil
1 c. day-old French bread,
   cut into cubes

1 clove garlic, crushed

Heat oil and garlic in a skillet. Add bread cubes and turn until browned.

Seen on a fortune cookie:
The first person you see
on Valentine's Day will be
your valentine.

Roasted Cornish Hens

Plump, tender hens, one for each of you, are easy, fun and delicious.

2 Rock Cornish Hens, approximately 1 lb. each
2 T. vegetable oil
salt, pepper and garlic powder to taste

Rub hens with oil and season inside and out. Roast in an uncovered roasting pan for approximately 1 hour, or until meat thermometer registers 180 degrees at inner thigh.

Make a love note jar for your family. Use a big, wide-mouthed pickle jar, and have each family member tuck one or two love notes into the jar about a week before Valentine's Day. (Don't forget to decorate the jar with ribbons, hearts and cupids!) On Valentine's Day, each person gets to draw a love note. The notes can vary from coupons to wash dishes and do laundry, to simple messages telling family members why you love them.

Have a valentine-making party. Serve heart cookies and pink punch after dinner, and have the entire family make cards for their special valentines. Let your imaginations run wild with glitter, glue and hearts! You'll be thrilled with your creations. A handmade valentine is always the most meaningful.

Filet Mignon Steaks Flambé

Tempt your love with the tenderest of steaks, marinated and seared to juicy perfection.

2-6 oz. filet mignon steaks,
   1 1/4" thick
1/4 c. Cognac
1 T. unsalted butter
1/2 T. vegetable oil

1/2 t. coarsely ground black
   pepper
2 large shallots, minced
1/4 c. beef broth
salt to taste

Forty-five minutes before cooking, sprinkle 1 tablespoon of the Cognac over the steaks and let stand at room temperature. In a heavy skillet, melt 1/2 tablespoon of the butter in the oil. Rub the steaks with the pepper. When the skillet is hot enough that a drop of water bounces off the surface, add the steaks. Cover partially and cook over high heat about 2 minutes, or until bottom is crusty. Turn and cook another 2 minutes on the other side. Reduce heat to medium and continue cooking about 2 minutes longer per side, turning once more. Transfer the steaks to a warm plate. Melt the remaining butter in the skillet with the oil, add the shallots, and cook over moderately high heat until shallots are translucent. Add the remaining Cognac to the skillet and ignite with a match. Cook over high until the flame extinguishes itself, about 30 seconds. Add the beef broth, stir, and boil until liquid is reduced to 1/4 cup. Spoon sauce over the steaks and sprinkle with salt to taste.

Find anything and everything heart-shaped that you own and create a Valentine's Day centerpiece. Use heart-shaped cookie cutters, pillows, sachets, or construction paper hearts. String red and pink ribbons throughout for a fun table setting.

Roasted Baby Red Potatoes

6 red new potatoes
2 T. olive oil
coarse salt, to taste

freshly ground black pepper
to taste
2 cloves garlic, minced
1 T. Italian parsley, chopped

Prick the potatoes with a fork and arrange on a baking sheet. Bake in a 350 oven for 1 1/2 hours. Cut into quarters and place in a warm bowl. Toss with the remaining ingredients.

Chocolate Puffs

1 sheet frozen puff pastry
6 oz. pkg. semi-sweet chocolate chips
1/4 c. walnuts, chopped
powdered sugar

Thaw pastry 30 minutes. Roll out on a lightly floured surface to a 12" square. Cut into four 6" squares. In the middle of each square, place 1/4 cup chocolate chips and 1 tablespoon walnuts. Bring all four corners of the pastry squares up above the chocolate, join the corners and twist. Fan out the corners. Place on an ungreased baking sheet and bake in preheated 425 degree oven for 10 to 15 minutes, or until golden brown. Let stand 10 minutes; sprinkle with powdered sugar.

Another simple, easy dessert is an Angel Cake. Make or buy a dreamy, white angel food cake...make it extra luscious with strawberry whipped cream filling, or drizzle with fresh raspberry sauce. Sprinkle with candy confetti or red hots for added sizzle.

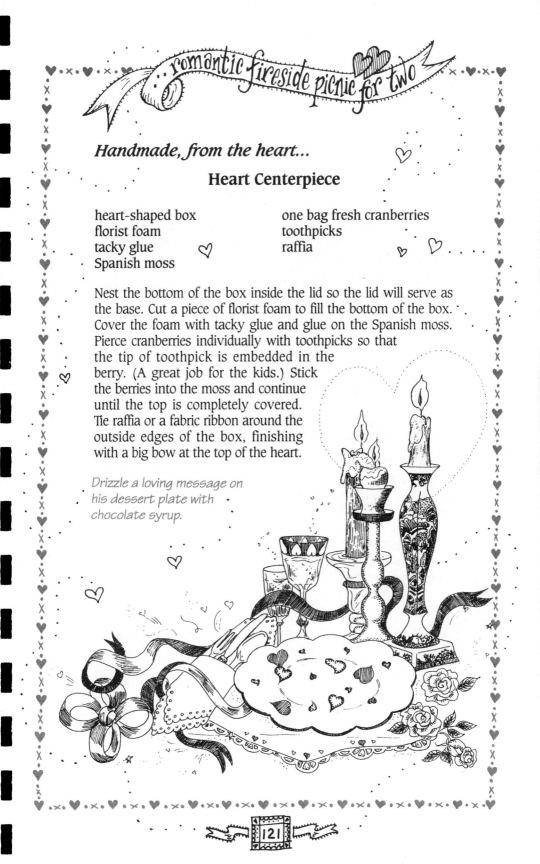

Handmade, from the heart...

Heart Centerpiece

heart-shaped box
florist foam
tacky glue
Spanish moss

one bag fresh cranberries
toothpicks
raffia

Nest the bottom of the box inside the lid so the lid will serve as the base. Cut a piece of florist foam to fill the bottom of the box. Cover the foam with tacky glue and glue on the Spanish moss. Pierce cranberries individually with toothpicks so that the tip of toothpick is embedded in the berry. (A great job for the kids.) Stick the berries into the moss and continue until the top is completely covered. Tie raffia or a fabric ribbon around the outside edges of the box, finishing with a big bow at the top of the heart.

Drizzle a loving message on his dessert plate with chocolate syrup.

Hearts Afire

Handmade Frame

Give your sweetie a new photo of yourself in a special frame. Purchase an unfinished wood frame and hand-paint it with glittery hearts using gold and silver metallic acrylic paints. You can add a sparkly French-wire ribbon attached with a glue gun. Or découpage old valentine cut-outs or stickers onto the frame by arranging cut-outs and brushing with several coats of découpage medium. Your valentine will love it!

Sweetheart Cookies

Make your favorite sugar cookie recipe; cut into heart shapes. Sprinkle with pink sugar crystals. Melt a handful of chocolate chips, or a solid chocolate candy bar, in a sealed plastic bag in the microwave. Snip off a tiny corner of the bag and make squiggly designs or write special secret messages to your loved ones. Put a cookie (or two) at each placesetting.

Make it Memorable

For this special occasion, dim the lights, bring out lots of candles and tie ribbons to the corners of your tablecloth. Use your best china and silver!

Index

Gooseberry Patch Originals

BUMBLEBEES & BUTTERFLIES

A garden Journal with plenty of space for all your garden-fresh recipes

HOMESPUN CHRISTMAS

A heartwarming collection of Christmas recipes, tips and ideas

SLEIGHBELLS & MISTLETOE

A Christmas Journal for jotting down all your best holiday ideas

TEACUPS & GINGERBREAD

A kitchen Journal for recording your favorite recipes & ideas

Gooseberry Patch Originals

WELCOME HOME for the HOLIDAYS
your companion from ★ September through December

OLD-FASHIONED COUNTRY COOKIES
hundreds of recipes, tips, & ideas

★**OLD-FASHIONED**★ **COUNTRY CHRISTMAS**
our all-time **BEST SELLER!**

GOOD FOR YOU!
recipes, fun ideas, heartwarming stories, good for body, mind, soul

FOR BEES & ME
garden-fresh recipes, backyard entertaining & gifts from the garden

GOOSEBERRY PATCH
P.O. Box 190, Dept. CELW
Delaware, OH 43015

A Country Store In Your Mailbox

♡ How to Order ♡
For faster service on credit card orders.
call toll-free 1-800-85-GOOSE!
(1-800-854-6673)

Please send me the following Gooseberry Patch books:

Book	Quantity	Price	Total
Old-Fashioned Country Christmas	————	$14.95	————
Welcome Home for the Holidays	————	$14.95	————
Old-Fashioned Country Cookies	————	$14.95	————
For Bees & Me	————	$17.95	————
Good For You!	————	$14.95	————
Homespun Christmas	————	$14.95	————
Celebrate Autumn	————	$12.95	————
Celebrate Winter	————	$12.95	————
		Merchandise Total	————
		Ohio Residents add 5 1/2%	————

Shipping & handling: Add $2 for each book. Call for special delivery prices.

Total ————

Quantity discounts and special shipping prices available when purchasing 6 or more books. Call and ask! Wholesale inquires invited.

Name: _____

Address: _____

City: _____ State: _____ Zip: _____

We accept checks, money orders, Visa or MasterCard (please include expiration date). Payable in U.S. funds only. Prices subject to change.

GOOSEBERRY PATCH
P.O. Box 190, Dept. CELW
Delaware, OH 43015

A Country Store In Your Mailbox

♡ How to Order ♡
For faster service on credit card orders.
call toll-free 1-800-85-GOOSE!
(1-800-854-6673)

Please send me the following Gooseberry Patch books:

Book	Quantity	Price	Total
Old-Fashioned Country Christmas	————	$14.95	————
Welcome Home for the Holidays	————	$14.95	————
Old-Fashioned Country Cookies	————	$14.95	————
For Bees & Me	————	$17.95	————
Good For You!	————	$14.95	————
Homespun Christmas	————	$14.95	————
Celebrate Autumn	————	$12.95	————
Celebrate Winter	————	$12.95	————
		Merchandise Total	————
		Ohio Residents add 5 1/2%	————

Shipping & handling: Add $2 for each book. Call for special delivery prices.

Total ————

Quantity discounts and special shipping prices available when purchasing 6 or more books. Call and ask! Wholesale inquires invited.

Name: _____

Address: _____

City: _____ State: _____ Zip: _____

We accept checks, money orders, Visa or MasterCard (please include expiration date). Payable in U.S. funds only. Prices subject to change.

brownies ♥ steamy mugs of cider ☺ gathering of friends

cranberry bread ❄ glittery gift-wraps ✱ simmering potpourri ♥ old fashioned gingerbread ✱

simmering stew-pots ☺ paper snowflakes ✱ chocolate fudge ♥ snowflakes on your nose ☺ picnics by the fire ✿ heavenly angels ♥ freshly-cut pine